iSyllabu
islam · iman · ihsan

One Year Diploma in Islamic Studies

Semester Three

Prayer 3: Returning to the Homeland - **Living the Law 2**: Case Studies -
Towards a Tranquil Soul 2: Spiritual Ailments and their Cures

© *2018 Ruzwan Mohammed.*

iSyllabus

Semester Three class notes

Page Number

Module 1

Understanding the law and spirituality of Prayer and Funeral rites

Lesson 6   *36*

In the shade of "Every innovation is a misguidance"

1. *Placing the discussion on Bid'ah in the proper context*

2. Prophetic traditions regarding innovation
2.1 Absolute Hadith
2.2 Qualified Hadith
2.3 Ground rules for understanding these Hadith

3. Language - The meaning of 'Every' (kull)
3.1 Conclusion on the meaning of 'every'

4. Definitions of Bidah

4.1 Al-Ghazzali
4.2 Qadi Abu Bakr ibn al-'Arabi al-Maliki
4.3 Imam Al-Nawawi
4.4 Badr al-Din Al-'Ayni al-Hanafi

5. Schools of Law and Bid'ah

6. Conditions of a good innovation

7. Innovations performed by early scholars that where not done by the Prophet ﷺ

8. The proofs of those that hold all bid'ah as blameworthy
8.1 That the religion is complete
8.2 'Every innovation is misguided'
8.3 The sayings of the Salaf

Module 2

Living the Law 2: Case Studies: Understanding the application of Islamic Law in the modern age

4. Music and *sama'*
    4.1 'Abdal Ghani an-Nablusi on *sama*

5. The legal schools on the prohibition of music
    5.1 Legal texts on singing and musical instruments

6. General conclusions
    6.1 The classical discussion...
    6.2 The contemporary discussion...

The issue of meat

1. Introduction
    1.1 Animal welfare issues
    1.2 Market forces

2. The Muslim law of halal meat [*dhabiha*]

3. The one slaughtering
    3.1 The religion of the one slaughtering.
    3.2 The pronouncement of the *tasmiyyah* (pronouncing bismillah)
    3.3 *Tasmiyyah* and machine slaughter

4. The severing of vital arteries.

5. That the animal be deemed alive at the time of slaughter.

6. Formal responses to the issue of stunning
    6.1 The joint Muslim World League/World Health Organization meeting.

Appendix

Zakat case study - the scope of "in the path of God" (fisibilillah)

1. The relevance of zakat in the modern age

2. What is the meaning of *fisibilillah*?
    2.1 The case of the majority
    2.2 The case of those that extend *fisibilillah* to all types of good
    2.3 The case of those that extend *fisibilillah* to include all forms of promoting Islam

3. General observations on the third position

The Ethics of war and the contemporary issue of Suicide bombings

1. The Just War

2. Contextual considerations - Leadership & Noncombatants
    2.1 Legitimate leadership
    2.2 Noncombatants

3. 'Suicide attacks'
    3.1 Modern dilemmas? The contemporary nature of suicide bombings
    3.2 Definitions and terms
    3.3 The proofs

4. Who is a *Shahid*?
    4.1 The Schools of law on the *Shahid*

Module 3

Towards a Tranquil Soul: The Spiritual Ailments of the Heart and their Cures

Returning to the Homeland

Understanding the law and spirituality of Prayer and Funeral rites

Module Fqh 4.05.D

Lesson 1
Significance of the Friday prayer

> ***Aims:*** To be able to understand the rulings related to the Friday prayer as well as the legal issues related to the Sermon (*khutbah*).
> **Objectives:**
> Having successfully completed this lesson, students should be able to demonstrate the ability to:
> [1] Discuss the importance and significance of Friday in the Muslim faith tradition.
> [2] Mention the ruling related to both the Friday prayer and the sermon that accompanies it.
> [3] List the conditions for correctly performing the Friday prayer.
> [4] Mention the Fard and Sunnah elements of the Friday sermon.
> [5] Describe the method of performing the Sermon.
> [6] Outline the issue of using non-Arabic as the language for delivering the *khutbah*.
> [7] List some of the etiquettes of the day of *Jumu'ah*.

1. Significance of Friday

> *"O you who believe! When the call for Friday prayer is made, hasten towards the remembrance of God and leave all transactions. This is best for you if only you knew" [62:9]*

> *Abu Hurayrah relates that the Messenger of God ﷺ said: "The best day that has seen the light of the sun is the day of Jumu'ah. It was on this day that Adam was created, he was granted entry into Paradise, it was on this day that he was removed from Paradise and it is on this day that he was expelled from it. The Hour will not fall on any day except Jumu'ah." [Muslim, 1977].*

> *The Messenger of God ﷺ said: "Jumu'ah is the most virtuous day that you have. It was on this day that Adam was created and passed away. On this day the trumpet will be blown and all will be struck unconscious. So send abundant blessings upon me on this day as this will be presented to me." The Companions asked: "O the Messenger of God! How will they be presented to you even as your bones have become like dust?" He replied: "God, the Most High and Glorious, has prohibited the earth from consuming the bodies of the Prophets." [Abu Dawud, 1047].*

2. The Ruling of the Friday Prayer (*Jumu'ah*)

> *The Messenger of God ﷺ said: "The person who misses out three Friday [prayers] out of dismissive negligence (tahawunan), God Most High puts a seal over their heart." [Tirmidhi].*

The prayer is a specific individual obligation (*fard 'ayn*) for the inhabitants of a city, the performance of which is more stressed than that for performing Dhuhr in congregation. There is a scholarly consensus that it consists of two rak'ah.

> *"The obligatory status of the prayer is established by the Qur'an and the Sunnah. The consensus of the Ummah is that the person who denies this falls outside the pale of Islam" [Ibn Humam, Fath-al-Qadir, Vol. I, p. 407].*

2.1 Exceptions to the rule

Children, women, travellers, the sick, as well as those that are blind or paralyzed are exempt from the ruling to attend the Friday prayer.

> *It is related in the prophetic tradition that the Messenger ﷺ said, "The Friday Prayer is obligatory for every Muslim, except the servant, woman, child and the sick." [Abu Daud].*

3. The conditions required for the correct performance of *Jumu'ah*
There are certain preconditions that have to be met before the *Jumu'ah* prayer can be performed (*shurut al-sihah*)[1]. Under normal circumstances, if any of these preconditions is lacking, the congregation will not be deemed to have been correct.

---

[1] *Ibn Humam, Fath al-Qadir, v2, pg 47-67*

3.1 That it is within a city or its environs

This means that the *Jumu'ah* is held in a population centre which is self-sufficient and caters for all the basic necessities of the population and has facilities such as security and a branch of the judiciary to settle disputes. Historically, it is related that the first *Jumu'ah* that was established after that in Madinah al-Munawwarah, was in the mosque of the tribe of Abd ul-Qays situated in *Jawathi*, which lies in Bahrain on the eastern seaboard of the Arabian peninsula [al-Bukhari, 892].

Areas attached to the city are also obliged to attend the prayer. *"Those living in the suburbs are duty bound, like the people of the city, to come and attend the Jumu'ah Prayer [Ibn Humam, Fath al-Qadir].*

3.2 It be under the auspices of the Muslim political authority

This was a condition for the correct performance of the *Jumu'ah* prayer in Muslim lands as it was important to retain a degree of political and spiritual unity. Therefore, independent congregations were not allowed to set up *Jumu'ah* prayers in opposition to a decree by the ruler. However, this condition is unattainable in non-Muslim lands and therefore, scholars are of the opinion that Muslims should establish congregations for the *Jumu'ah* prayer in their own localities as the need arises.

3.3 It be performed within the time of *Dhuhr*.

This means that both the sermon (*khutbah*) and the prayer take place after the time of *Dhuhr* has entered.

> Salama ibn al-Awka' said: *"We would pray Jumu'ah with the Prophet ﷺ when the sun had passed the meridian, and when we returned [home], we could still trace our shadow."* [Muslim].

3.4 There is a congregation of three or more with the Imam for the prayer

The number required for the prayer to be valid is 3 or more people attending the prayer who fulfill the conditions of acting as an Imam *[Ibn Abidin, Hashiyyah, v1, 545]*.

3.5 Open access to the prayer area

As the *Jumu'ah* prayer is one the outward symbols of Islamic faith it should be performed in a manner that shows its all inclusive nature. Therefore, congregations that are closed to certain people and specific to one group, are not recognized as the *Jumu'ah* in normal circumstances.

> It is narrated that Ibn Abbas said, *"The Prophet ﷺ was given permission to establish the Jumu'ah congregation before he migrated to Madinah, but he was unable to bring together people in Makkah for this task [due to the hostile environment at the time] and therefore, he wrote to Musab ibn Umayr [that he establish it in Madinah]."* [See al-Suhayli, Rawd al-'Unf, v4, pg 54-6]

3.6 The Sermon (*Khutbah*)

> *"O you who believe, when the call to prayer is proclaimed on the day of Jumu'ah, hasten to the remembrance of God." [Jumu'ah:9]*

The Khutbah (sermon) is an essential condition for the correct performance of *Jumu'ah* prayer and is made up of elements that are essential (*fard*) as well as sunnah. According Sa'id ibn Mussayib, the words in the verse of Qur'an *'the remembrance of God'* refer to the sermon given by the Imam. *[al-Tabari, v22, pg 624]*

4. What does the Khutbah consist of?

The Khutbah consist of two short sermons punctuated with a short sitting between them and they are to be delivered before the *Jumu'ah* prayer itself. As with all actions of the prayer, there are bare essential elements by which the minimum required for *Jumu'ah*, is fulfilled, as well as sunnah and recommend acts.

4.1 Fard element of the sermon

According to Abu Hanifah, absolute bare minimum without which the sermon is invalid, is the length of one *tasbih*, though even this is barely deemed sufficient as it is reprehensible to do so. It is more prudent for the minimum to be taken as the length of the *tashahud* in prayer.

4.2 Sunnah elements of the sermon

> *Jabir ibn Samurah said, "The Prophet* ﷺ *would not make his reminder during the Friday prayer too long, but rather it would be a few words." [al-Bukhari]*

It is the prophetic norm for there to be two sermons for *Jumu'ah* performed before the prayer itself, punctuated with a short sitting between them. Ibn Umar relates *"that the Messenger* ﷺ *used to deliver two sermons between which he would sit for a while." [al-Bukhari, 928]*

These should include:[2]
(a) Praising God in both sermons *[Hamd]*
(b) Invoking blessings on the Prophet ﷺ in both sermons *[Salawat]*
(c) Exhortation and advice for the congregation in both sermons *[Wasiyyah]*
(d) The recitation of at least one verse from the Qur'an in one of the two sermons *[Qira'ah]*
(e) A supplication for the believers in the final sermon *[Dua]*

4.3 Method of performing the Khutbah

> *Jabir ibn Samurah said "The Messenger of God* ﷺ *would deliver his Khutbah standing, would sit in between the two sermons, recite some verses of the Qur'an and then would remind people concerning the rights of God" [Muslim].*

When the Imam comes to the pulpit (*minbar*), the Muezzin should perform the adhan in front of him while the Imam is seated facing the congregation.
Once the adhan has been completed, the Imam stands and delivers the first of the two sermons.

4.3.1 First Khutbah

The Imam should stand and silently recite seeking refuge from the Shaytan (*audhubillah...*). He should then start the khutbah with the praise of God, mention the two testimonies of faith and send prayers and benedictions on the Prophet ﷺ after which he should remind people of their obligations to piety *[taqwa]* and recite from the Qur'an, even if it be one verse finishing with the main sermon topic.

4.3.2 Second khutbah

It is sunnah to repeat the praising of God as well as prayers on the Prophet ﷺ at the beginning of this *khutbah* after which one should supplicate with what is seen fit and pray for the Muslims. It is also recommended to express God's pleasure *[rida]* for the Companions (r.a.) of the Prophet ﷺ especially the four *khulafah* before the *dua*.

4.4 The language of the Khutbah[3]

The language in which the two sermons have been delivered has always been Arabic, even when Islam spread in countries where the natives did not understand what was being said. Recently, there has been a move towards delivering part of the sermons in local languages, especially in the West, where it is one of the rare opportunities one gets to educate and convey important lessons to those that may otherwise be on the periphery of the observant Muslim community.

---

[2] These are considered essential according to the Shafi'i school of law *[al-Shurbini, Mughni al-Muhtaj v1, pg426-8]*, whereas the Maliki school consider the minimum length to be approximated by comparing it to any speech delivered in a gathering to bring attention to a point. This is what is referred to in Arabic as being a '*sermon*'. The minimum length according to the Maliki school is therefore longer than that mentioned by the Hanafi school above *[Ibn Hajib, Jami' al-Ummahat, pg 123, al-Dasuqi, Sharh al-Kabir, v1, pg 592]*. Ideally, the Imam should ensure that the sermon is correct according to all schools of law.

[3] The Maliki school hold that "*...the sermon can only be delivered, in Arabic even if the whole congregation is non Arabic speaking. If there is none that can deliver the khutbah in Arabic, they are not obliged to pray Jumah*" *[al-Dasuqi, Sharh al-Kabir, v1, pg 592]*. The Shafi'i school hold that the five integrals mentioned above have to be in Arabic, with later scholars in the school stating that non-Arabic may be used in the khutbah as long as the essentials are delivered in Arabic *[al-Ramil, Nihayat al-Muhtaj, v7, 82]*. The Hanbali school permit the whole khutbah to be delivered in a non-Arabic language if there is no one competent to deliver it in Arabic *[Kashaf al-Qina', al-Bahuti, v2, pg 642]*. According to Abu Hanifah it is not a condition that the *khutbah* be in Arabic even if the Imam is able to do so, though it is reprehensible to do so. *[Ibn Abidin, Hashiyyah, v1, pg 147]*

As most people only attend for the time of the actual sermon and not for the summary translation of the sermon given before or after the prayer, whether all or part of the sermon can be given in other than Arabic has been debated by various Fiqh Councils in the Muslim world. The issues are summarized below.

> *"Some scholars regard the khutbah as salah or part of the salah and, because of this, make it a condition that the khutbah be in Arabic. According to Abu Hanifah, Arabic is not a condition for the khutbah[4]; one is allowed to give it in any language. By way of reconciling both opinions, many jurists of our time assert that in an Arab land and wherever people understand Arabic the whole khutbah should be delivered in Arabic. But in a non-Arab land where most people do not understand Arabic, the sermon part [5] of the khutbah should be done in the language of the people, because there is no use of a sermon if people do not understand it. The rest of it [6], however, should be said in Arabic"*
> *[Nadawi, al-Fiqh al-Islami, pg 212-213, endorsed by members of the Islamic Fiqh Academy in its seminar in Jeddah on 8-16th Rabi al-Thani 1402 AH].*

5. Etiquette, rules and preparations

> *Abu Hurayrah said that the Prophet ﷺ said, "If you say to your companion 'Be silent' during Jumu'ah and the Imam is performing the sermon then you have engaged in idle talk" [Bukhari, 394].*

5.1 It is preferred that the person addressing the congregation *(khatib)* also be the Imam for the prayer, though it is allowed that the task of Imam be delegated to another.

5.2 It is prohibited to talk or perform sunnah or nafl prayers in the period when the Imam delivers the sermon until the end of the prayer.

5.3 Any type of dhikr or invocations of blessings *[Salawat]* done should be silent.

5.4 One unable to hear the sermon may occupy themselves in a way that does not distract others, remaining consistent with the prohibition regarding speech during the sermon.

5.5 It is reprehensible for somebody to travel on the day of *Jumu'ah* after midday before performing the Jum'ah prayer without an excuse.

5.6 It is an emphasized sunnah that one prays four rakat before the *Jumu'ah* prayer as well as four afterwards.

5.7 Whoever misses the *Jumu'ah* prayer should pray Dhuhr in its place.

5.8 It is forbidden for somebody who has no excuse not to attend the *Jumu'ah* to perform the Dhuhr prayer before people have completed the *Jumu'ah*.

5.9 An individual who has an excuse not to attend the *Jumu'ah* is recommended to delay the performance of Dhuhr until after the *Jumu'ah* prayer has been performed *[See al-Shurunbalali, Maraqih].*

6. General preparations for the day of Jumu'ah

> *Abdullah (ibn Umar) reported from his father that while he was addressing the people on Friday (sermon), a person, one of the Companions of the Messenger of God ﷺ, entered (the mosque). 'Umar said to him loudly: What kind of hour is this (for attending the prayer)? He said: I was busy today and I did not return to my house when I heard the call (to Friday prayer), and I did no more than perform ablution. Upon this 'Umar said: Just ablution! You know that the Messenger of God ﷺ commanded to take a bath" [Muslim, 1836].*

> *Abu Sa'id al-Khudri reports that the Prophet ﷺ said: "Whoever recites Surah al-Kahf on Jumu'ah will have illumination from light from one Jumu'ah to the next" [an-Nasa'i].*

---

[4] See footnote above on the position of Abu Hanifah.

[5] The *'sermon part'* of the khutbah refers to the main part of the khutbah dealing with the central message including exhortation and advice for the congregation.

[6] This refers to the essential introduction and testification to faith, Quranic verse and prayer on the Prophet ﷺ etc.

Lesson 2
Traveller prayer [1] - Shortening the prayer *(Qasr)*

Aims: To understand the rulings related to the traveller in as much as this relates to the dispensation to shorten one's prayers.

Objectives:
Having successfully completed this lesson, students should be able to demonstrate the ability to:
[1] Discuss the basic prayer rulings that are outlined for the traveller.
[2] Mention the ruling of shortening the prayers.
[3] Outline the condition for one to be classified as a traveller.
[4] Mention the period for which one remains classified as a traveller in the sacred law.
[5] Explain what is meant by *'permanent abode'* and the ruling related to this classification?
[6] Explain what is meant by *'temporary abode'* and the ruling related to this classification?
[7] Use knowledge of these classifications to solve various scenarios encountered while travelling.
[8] Mention the ruling of praying behind an Imam who is a classed as a traveller and vice versa.
[9] Explain what is meant by *Du'a'* and whether these are always answered.

1. The prayer of the Traveller (*Al-Musafir*)

> *"And when you go forth in the land there is no sin upon you, if you shorten your prayer when you fear the disbelievers may attack you." [al-Nisa, 101]*

This verse, even though it relates directly to the manner of performing the prayer when in fear of attack, is taken by scholars to extend to the permissibility of shortening one's prayers while travelling.

> *Aishah said: "The prayer was made an obligation in Makkah in sets of two rak'ah. When the Prophet ﷺ came to Medina, two rak'ah were added to each prayer except for maghrib because it is the witr (odd prayer) of the daytime, and Fajr due to its lengthy recitation. So when one travels, one performs the original prayer" [Ahmad].*

> *Ya'la ibn Umayyah said: "I asked 'Umar "Explain to me why people shorten the prayer while God has said, **And when you go forth...**" and those days are gone now!' 'Umar said: 'I wondered about that too and I mentioned that to the Prophet ﷺ and he said: 'This is a charity that God, the Exalted, has bestowed upon you, so accept His charity'" [al-Nasai].*

2. The ruling and conditions of shortening the Prayer

It is obligatory (*wajib*) that the prayers be shortened for Dhuhr, 'Asr and Isha to two rakats[7].

2.1 When is a person considered a 'traveller'?

A person upon leaving their permanent residence and passing beyond the city limits with the intention of travelling around 48 miles.

2.2 How long does a person remain a traveller?

The person remains classified as a traveller as long as they are

2.2.1 Engaged in travel thereafter until they ***return back*** to their permanent residence
2.2.2 In a place of temporary residency and intend to stay ***less*** than 15 days
2.2.3 In a place where one's residency is ***uncertain***. This is when one is unsure of the length of stay and may have to travel at any time, even if this uncertainty extends beyond 15 days.

---

[7] If one does not shorten the prayers the rulings regarding having left out shortening the prayer is the same as leaving any *wajib* act, therefore the general rules regarding apply here. If one did not shorten the prayer while traveling out of forgetfulness it is necessary to perform the prostration of forgetfulness at the end of the prayer. However if one shortened one's prayer intentionally, then one must repeat the prayer. Travellers may pray sunnah prayers if they find it easy to do so, and are afforded dispensation not to if pre-occupied with actual travel.

> *Nafi'i relates that Ibn 'Umar was held up in Azerbaijan for six months, due to snow blocking the mountain-pass, and he prayed two rak'ah." Similarly, Hafs ibn 'Ubaidullah reports: "Anas ibn Malik stayed in al-Sham [Greater Syria] for two years and he prayed the prayer of a traveller."*

3. Permanent and temporary residency

The sacred law recognizes two different types of abode with regards to the concession to shorten the prayer.

The first is a **permanent abode,** which is either one's home town or where one has moved permanently for marriage[8] or work[9].

The second is a **temporary abode** - any non-permanent place of residency where one needs to stay for a period over 15 days regardless of the reason, such as work or pleasure.

> *"It is related from Ibn 'Umar that he said "Whoever stays in a place for 15 day should start to perform their prayer in a complete manner." [al-Tirmidhi, 548].*

> *"Imran ibn Hussain states "I left on the expedition with the Prophet ﷺ in the year of conquest and we stayed in Mecca for eighteen nights and we only prayed two rakats." Ibn Abbas said "The Prophet ﷺ stayed in Makkah in the year of the conquest for 15 days shortening the prayer..." Al-Thawri and the scholars of Kufa took as a proof [for their view] the narration regarding fifteen days on account of it being the lowest number related in this context and interpreted anything over this as not being contradictory to the lower number." [Ibn Hajr, Fath al-Bari, v2, pg 562; Ibn Arabi, Aridah al-Ahwadhi, v3, pg 18-19].*

3.1 Permanent residency ruling.

One always prays the prayer in full *unless the status of permanency changes.*

3.1.1 When does one's permanent status change?

A person's place of residence only stops being one's *permanent* abode when one intends to move permanently.

> *"A permanent abode, where a person was born or married into, is replaced by another if the person takes up residence in another place since the Messenger ﷺ and his Companions who emigrated with him shortened their prayers when they returned to Mecca even though it used to be their original home. This is on account of the fact that they had made Medina their new residence." [Ibn Humam, Fath al-Qadir, v2, pg 43].*

Scenario

Khalid is born in Aberdeen so prays his prayers there in full. He later moves to Glasgow for work and marries there as well. If Khalid now visits Aberdeen he would shorten his prayers.

3.2 Temporary residency ruling

3.2.1 A traveller will not become a temporary resident until he firmly intends to stay at a place for a period of fifteen days. The duration of the concession starts from the time one makes this intention.

3.2.2 One prays the full prayer until one travels from the temporary residency.

---

[8] If one has a spouse in another city that is more than the distance of ±48 miles and visits the spouse with no intention to remain for more than 15 days, some scholars state that one can shorten the prayers while others say you cannot *[Ibn Humam, Fath al-Qadir, v2, pg 41; Ibn Abidin, Hashiyyah, v2, pg 135].*

[9] If a person commutes for work each day for a distance above the limit to be considered a traveller, they are given the dispensation to shorten the prayers until they return into boundary of their city.

3.2.3 The intention of staying fifteen days has to be for staying the full fifteen days at one place. If one is commuting between a number of population centers, one will be considered a traveller in all those places.[10]

3.2.4 When does one's temporary status change?

3.2.4.1 A temporary place of residence ceases to be so simply if one travels from it.

Scenario

Ahmed is a Liverpudlian and went to Newcastle to see his uncle with the intention of remaining 20 days. He will not shorten his prayers during that time.
He starts the journey home, but having left Newcastle, he has to return back to pick up something he forgot, and intends to stay another couple of days. He will shorten his prayers during this extra period as a temporary place of residence ceases to be so simply if one travels from it.

4. The traveller praying behind a resident and vice versa

If a traveller comes upon a congregation of residents praying, they join the prayer and complete the prayer as residents would without shortening the prayer. This is regardless of whether the congregation is for a prayer prayed on time or not. It is related by Imran Ibn Hussain that the Prophet ﷺ prayed two rakat whilst in Mecca and then said *"O people of Mecca! complete your prayers for we are travelling" [At-Tirmidhi].*

4.1 If one missed prayers while travelling, they are made up shortened after arriving home just as they would be prayed if one was a traveller and vice versa.

5. Praying in trains, planes and automobiles

Obligatory prayers done while travelling in vehicles that are moving still need to be performed within their time with due consideration to the performance of the pillars.

If performing the pillars is not possible due to the vehicle not stopping within the time of the prayer or lack of space, one prays in the manner outlined in the prayer of the sick, taking due consideration for one's safety as well as that of other passengers.[11]

> It is related that the Prophet ﷺ said *"There are three for whom their supplications are answered and there is no doubt therein; the supplication of the parent, the traveller and of the one oppressed." [Abu Dawud 1536].*

6. Reconnecting with the Spirit - What is Du'a?

> **"When My servants ask you concerning Me, I am indeed close, responding to the prayer of supplicant when he calls upon on Me." [2: 186]**

> *"Dua is the servant beseeching God for grace ('inayyah) and the provision of help. Its reality is the demonstration of one's deep-rooted need towards God, divesting oneself of all power and capacity. This is the mark of utter servant-hood and feeling of the fragility of one's human nature. It encapsulates the meaning of praising God as well as ascribing favor and generosity to Him. It is on account of this that The Prophet ﷺ said "Dua' is the essence of worship" [at-Tirmidhi, 2969][al-Khattabi, Sha'n al-Dua, pg 4].*

7. Are supplications always answered?

> *"If one were to enquire as to the meaning of His words **"Supplicate Me and I will answer to you" [Ghafir: 60]**, as it is a promise from God which should be fulfilled and it is not permitted that there be any departure from this [promise, then how should we understand this?] (...)*

---

[10] If one is travelling in a family (such as a husband and wife) or as a group, the decision of whether one is considered as travelling or not is delegated to the leader or one vested with deciding upon one's movements. However if there is no clear information forthcoming in this regard, one is considered as being alone. Therefore in such a situation, whether one shortens the prayer or not depends on one's own circumstances and not those of the group.

[11] Some scholars state that the prayer should be performed again later once one is able to fulfill the essential elements of the prayer.

*It is said that this promise is conditional on God's Will (mashi'ah), as in His words **'It is He who you call on and, if He wills, He will deliver you from whatever it was that made you call on Him." [6:41].***

Indeed, words can be found in a general form while what is intended [by them] is a specific set of affairs. [Meaning] that what is answered of supplications is that which corresponds with the Ultimate Decree [Qada], since clearly not all those who supplicate can see a response to their supplication. This shows that [the verse] refers to a specific situation with known variables.

*It is also said that the meaning of **"answering"** here is that the one that supplicates will receive a response of one kind or another in return for the supplication. This may be, if it corresponds to the Ultimate Decree [Qada], in the form of a speedy response to the dua made.*

If the decree is not favorable in this regard, then the person is granted a degree of tranquility in their soul, as well as an expansion of their breast. This, together with a patience through which one is able to bear the burdens that will inevitability pass their way. When all is said and done, the prayer is not devoid of benefit. This itself is a type of response or answer.

It is related that Abu Hurayrah said that the Prophet ﷺ said "There is no servant that turns their face to God, May He be Exalted, and asks of Him a request, except that he is given it, either hastened for him in this world, or else stored for him in the Hereafter on the condition that the person does not become hasty. They enquired "How does he become hasty?" He said 'That the person say 'I supplicated and supplicated and I do not see a response to me." (Ahmed 2/448) [al-Khattabi, Sha'n ad-Dua, 12-13].

Lesson 3
Traveller prayer [2] - Joining the prayers (*jam'a*)

> **Aims:** To be able to understand the prophetic traditions related to the combining of prayers as well as the significance of Supplication (*Dua'*) in Muslim worship.
>
> **Objectives:**
> Having successfully completed this lesson, students should be able to demonstrate the ability to:
> [1] Discuss the issue of combining the prayer with specific reference to the Prophetic hadith.
> [2] Outline the different legal schools on the issue of combining prayers.
> [3] Discuss the status of the hadith *"The Prophet ﷺ combined the prayers of Dhuhr and 'Asr together while in Medina on account of neither fear nor travelling"*
> [4] Mention the opinions of scholars on this hadith using the summary provided by Imam al-Nawawi.
> [5] Mention what scholars have stated on the prerequisite conditions for a supplication being accepted.
> [6] List, with the use of examples, the four factors that help in the acceptance of a supplication.

Text in Focus -
Interpreting a hadith regarding the Combining of Prayers

1. Joining the prayers when travelling

While Scholars have agreed as to the permissibility of **shortening (*qasr*)** one's prayers while travelling, they have differed as to whether it is permitted to **join two prayers together (*jam'*)**.

1.1 The Majority of Scholars have allowed people to join two prayers together when travelling the distance for which a person qualifies as a traveller in Islamic law.

1.2 The Hanafi school restrict joining prayers to the time of the Hajj, as the Prophet ﷺ is reported as having always prayed prayers in their own times. They explain all hadith quoted by the majority on this issue as examples where it appeared that the prayer was being combined *"apparent combining"* (jam' al-suwari) and not *"real combining"* (jam' al-haqiqi).

This position is based on the fact that we are told to make every prayer on time, while it is reported by Ibn Masud that the Prophet ﷺ never combined the prayers together except in Arafat and Muzdalifah during the Hajj period.

> *"Al-Shafi'i as well as the majority of scholars state that it is permissible to join between the Dhuhr and 'Asr prayer within the time of any of the two one wishes as well as between Maghrib and Isha in the time of any of the two one wishes, if this occurs during a long journey. Regarding the permissibility of this during a shorter journey, there are two narrations related from Al-Shafi'i, the more correct of which is that it is not permitted..."*
>
> *Abu Hanifah said "It is not permitted to join between two prayers on account of travelling, rain, illness or any other reason except in between Dhuhr and 'Asr in Arafat and between Maghrib and Isha in Muzdalifah due to the sacred rites [of Hajj]..." [an-Nawawi, al-Minhaj]*

2. Joining prayers when not travelling

Scholars have differed whether it is permitted to join prayers for a reason other than travelling. The pivotal hadith related to this discussion is that related in the collection of Imam Muslim that Ibn Abbas said:

> *"The Prophet ﷺ combined the prayers of Dhuhr and 'Asr while in Madinah on account of neither fear nor travelling. Abu Zubair said 'I asked Sa'id why he did this?' He said 'I asked Ibn Abbas the same thing and he said "He did not want to make things difficult for anybody from his community."' [Muslim]*

2.1 Points of interest in the hadith of Ibn Abbas

2.1.1 The hadith is a report of an action that the Prophet ﷺ performed with no explanation in his words as to why it was done. We are therefore left to provide a reason why the Prophet ﷺ joined the prayers in this manner. One explanation, from one of the most illustrious Companions, Ibn Abbas is given in the narration itself.

2.1.2 Ibn Abbas, is known amongst scholars to be the most accommodating of the companions in fiqh ruling. How did scholars deal with his explanation: *"He did not want to make things difficult for anybody from his community.'*?

The section below from al-Nawawi's commentary on the aforementioned hadith provides an interesting look into the manner of resolving this question and the manner in which scholars interpret the same religious text in different ways.

2.2 al-Nawawi's commentary on the hadith

"Scholars have provided various interpretations to this hadith. Imam al-Tirmidhi said at the end of his book 'There is no hadith in this book of mine that the community has agreed on not acting upon, except for the hadith of Ibn Abbas related to '[the Prophet ﷺ] combining prayers in Medina on account of neither fear nor rain' and the hadith regarding killing one who drinks wine for a fourth occasion."

What al-Tirmidhi says regarding the [ruling of the] hadith of he that drinks wine is indeed true, the hadith is abrogated as is indicated by Scholarly consensus (Ijma'). As for the hadith of Ibn Abbas scholars have agreed upon leaving acting upon the hadith, rather they have different opinions in this regard.

2.2.1 [On excuse of rain]

There are those *that interpret it as him ﷺ having joined the prayers due to the excuse of rain. This is well known from a group of earlier senior scholars but it is weak due to the narration 'on account of neither fear nor rain.'*

2.2.2 [Due to overcast conditions]

There are those *that have interpreted it as referring to overcast conditions. He ﷺ prayed Dhuhr after which the cloudiness disappeared and it became apparent that the time of 'Asr had entered and so he prayed it. **This is also incorrect** because even if there is a possibility of this happening for Dhuhr and 'Asr, there is no such possibility with regards to Maghrib and Isha.' [see also al Mazari, al-Mu'lim bi Fawa'id Muslim, 1/298].*

2.2.3 [A case of "apparent combining" (Jam' al-Suwari)]

There are others *that interpreted it as delaying the first prayer up until the last portion of its time at which time it is allowed. Upon completing it, the time for the second prayer starts and so it is then prayed as well. The prayers, therefore, were combined outwardly in appearance only. **This is also a weak** or rejected position, because it goes against the outward wording of the hadith in a way that is improbable. What Ibn Abbas did while he was giving a sermon [delaying the prayer past its time] and his taking proof from this hadith to back up his actions, as well as the validation from Abu Hurayrah of his explanation and not denouncing him, is clear in rejecting this interpretation.*

2.2.4 [due to illness or other excuses]

There are those *that say it is to be interpreted as combining prayers on account of illness or similar excuses. This is position of Ahmad ibn Hanbal as well as Al-Qadi Hussain. This has been chosen by Al-Khattabi and Al-Mutawali and Al-Ruyani from amongst our companions [i.e Shafi'i scholars]. **This is the preferred interpretation** for the outward meaning of the hadith in light of the actions of Ibn Abbas and the agreement of Abu Hurayrah on this. The difficulty in such a situation is more pronounced than during the time of rain.*

2..2.5 [On account of a legitimate need as long as it does not become a habit.]

A group *of Imams have taken the position of permitting the combining of prayers while not travelling if it is due to a legitimate need [as long as] the person does not make it a habit. This is a position of Ibn Sirin and 'Ashab from the companions of Imam Malik. Al-Khattabi has* related this from al-Qaffal and Al-Shashi al-Kabir from amongst the companions of Al-Shafi'i as well as Abu Is'haq al-Mirwazi amongst a group of the people of hadith. This was the chosen option of Ibn al-Mundhir.

This is supported by the apparent meaning of Ibn Abbas when he said 'He 🙏 intended to not make things difficult for his community', and he did not give the reason of illness or anything else and God knows best." [al-Nawawi, Sharh Muslim]

3. Reconnecting with the Spirit

3.1 The conditions of an accepted supplication

Abu Hurayrah relates that the Messenger of God 🙏 said: "God the Almighty is pure and accepts only that which is pure, and He has commanded the faithful to do that which He commanded the Messengers, and the Almighty has said: "O Messengers, eat of the good things and act righteously" [23:51]. God the Almighty has said: "O you who believe! Eat of the pure things We have provided you." Then he 🙏 mentioned a man who, having journeyed far, is disheveled, dusty and spreads out his hands to the heavens crying: "O Lord! O Lord!" yet his food is unlawful, his drink is unlawful, his clothing is unlawful, and he is nourished unlawfully, so how can his supplication be answered!" [Muslim].

The Prophet 🙏 said *"Supplicate to God in a state that you are certain that your supplication will be responded to, and know that God does not respond to a supplication that originates from a negligent, inattentive heart." [al-Tirmidhi]*

"Supplication and the prayers through which one seeks God's help are like a weapon. A weapon is only as good as the person who is making use of it; it is not merely a matter of how sharp it is. If the weapon is perfect, the arm of the one using it is strong, and there is nothing holding him back, then he can overcome the enemy. If any of these are wanting the resultant outcome will also be lacking" [Ibn al-Qayyim, al-Da'a wa'l-Dawa', p. 35].

*"Amongst the conditions of supplications is that they come from a servant accompanied with **a sincere intention** and **a display of abject poverty and need, destitution, while in a state of humility and awe.***

*The person supplicating should be in a state of **ritual purity**, **facing the Qiblah** and start the supplication with **praise of God** as well as sending **prayers on the Prophet** 🙏. Amongst the sunnah acts of the dua' is that one **raise one's hands** with palms spread open uncovered of clothing or any other covering. It is reprehensible to use an excessively loud voice..." [al-Khattabi, Sh'an al-Dua, 13-14].*

4. Factors that help in acceptance of a supplication

It is related by Abu Hurayrah that the Messenger of God 🙏 said: *'**There is an hour on Friday which if a Muslim finds it while praying and asks something from God, He will meet his request.**' He then indicated the shortness of that particular time with his hands." [al-Bukhari, 935].*

There are a number of Qur'anic verses and Prophetic traditions that indicate the underlying reasons due to which supplications are accepted. This usually goes back to one of four things:

4.1 The meritoriousness and blessing of the time.

Prophetic traditions point to the blessedness of certain times. These include the time between the adhan and the iqamah; just before dawn; during an hour of *Jumu'ah*; the month of Ramadan; during prostration; during the midst of battle; on the day of Arafat, upon the death of a person as well as many others.

Amr ibn Absha' narrated that the Prophet 🙏 said: "The closest any worshipper can be to His Lord is during the last part of the night, so if you can be amongst those who remember God at that time, then do so." [at-Tirmidhi,].

Umm Salamah narrated that, when Abu Salamah had just passed away, and had closed his eyes, the Prophet 🙏 said "Do not ask for yourselves anything but good, for the angels will say 'Amin' to all that you ask for. O Allah, forgive Abu Salamah, and raise his ranks among those who are guided." [Muslim].

The Messenger of God ﷺ said *"The best supplication is the supplication on the day of Arafat."* [Malik]

Sa'id ibn al-Musayyib narrates that 'Umar said *"Supplication is suspended between the heavens and the earth and no part of it is taken up until you send blessings upon your Prophet ﷺ.'* [al-Tirmidhi § 486].

Abu Umamah narrated that God's Messenger ﷺ was asked, O Messenger of God, which of supplications are heard, he said *"At the end of the night and upon the completion of the obligatory prayer."* [al-Tirmidhi].

4.2 The meritoriousness of the place.

It is related that Hasan al-Basri wrote a letter to the people of Mecca mentioning the 15 places where supplications are accepted there. Al-Shawkani says in a chapter relating to places of acceptance which are blessed spots *"I know of no proof regarding this except for what has been related from the Prophet ﷺ by Imam At-Tabarani with a strong chain of narration: 'supplications are accepted upon first sighting the Ka'bah.'*

4.3 A special state quality in the person supplicating.

This means that there are certain individuals who due to of the state or position that God has put them are privileged in having their supplication more likely to be answered.

It is related that the Prophet ﷺ said *"There are three people whose supplications are answered and there is no doubt therein; the supplication of the parent, the traveller and the one oppressed." [Abu Dawud 1536].*

It is also related that the Prophet ﷺ said *"There are three whose supplication is never rejected; the one fasting until he breaks the fast, the just ruler, and the supplication of the oppressed." [At-Tirmidhi 3668].*

It is also recommended to gather to supplicate as it is related from Habib ibn Muslimah that the Prophet ﷺ said *"No people come together with some of them supplicating and the others proclaiming 'Amin' except that God answers them." [Al-Hakim, 3/347].*

Similarly supplicating profusely at times of ease as indicated in the hadith *"Whoever would like to be well pleased to have their supplications answered at times of hardship and difficultly, let them supplicate profusely at times of ease." [at-Tirmidhi, 3379].*

The Prophet ﷺ said *"The supplication of a person for his brother behind his back is answered. He has an angel at his head overseeing him and every time he prays for his brother with something good, it says 'Amin, and may you have like of it.'" [Muslim, 2732].*

There are many other individuals that have been mentioned as having their prayers accepted in Prophetic hadith, such as **"a pious son"** [Bukhari 5974]; **"a person expelled from the corridors of power"** [Muslim 2622]. Similar hadith are related with regards to those that are performing **Hajj and Umra.**

4.4 The blessing of the supplication itself.

This means that the words through which God is beseeched and supplicated are themselves inherently blessed. It is related by Abu 'Umamah that the Prophet ﷺ said *"The greatest name of God which if He is called on by He responds is contained in the three chapters of Al-Baqarah, al-Imran and Ta-Ha." [Ibn Majah 3856].*

Lastly, it is related that from the etiquette of supplication is that one precedes it with a good action. Imam al-Zabidi says:

"From amongst its etiquette is that one precede it with a prayer as is mentioned by al-Halimi. He used as a support for this the fact that the Messenger ﷺ did this when he supplicated for

*his community in Quba and also from the words of God **'And when you have finished be firm and seek out your Lord' [94:8]**. In other words, when you have finished from your own prayer then extend yourself in supplication. Al-Zarkashi stated that this is why the supplication for rainfall is preceded by prayer, fasting, and charity." [al-Zabidi, Ithaf, 5/41].*

Lesson 4
Death and the funeral prayer

> ***Lesson Four Aims:*** To understand the practical and theoretical issues that arise when someone dies and how to navigate them.
> ***Objectives:***
> Having successfully completed this lesson, students should be able to demonstrate the ability to:
> 1. **Outline** what one should do when someone is approaching death.
> 2. **Explain** what is meant by the word '*talqin*' and when this can be done.
> 3. **Summarize** what is done immediately after a person passes away.
> 4. **Mention** when and how condolence is done.
> 5. **Explain** whether donating acts of charity and supplication for the dead is permitted.
> 6. **Mention** the opinion of scholars regarding the permissibility or otherwise of donating the reward of Quranic recitation to the dead.

"Every human being is bound to taste death: but only on the Day of Resurrection will you be requited in full [for whatever you have done] – whereupon he that shall be drawn away from the fire and brought into paradise will indeed have triumphed: for the life of this world is nothing but an enjoyment of self-delusion." [3:185]

1. Facing death with Fear and Hope

The final chapters of prayer are not concerned with what is performed by the person themselves but rather by other people on his or her behalf. This is done upon the death of an individual, where the congregation of Muslims are obliged to establish a special prayer before the deceased is placed in the grave, their final resting place which will either be *'a garden from the gardens of Paradise or a pit from the pits of Hell'*. The best thing that can be prepared by a person in advance of this is genuine awareness of God (*taqwa*).

> *Anas narrated that the Prophet* 🌸 *went to see a young man who was on his deathbed. The Prophet* 🌸 *asked him 'How are you?' The young man said, 'I have hope in God and fear Him.' The Prophet* 🌸 *said, "These two things never gather in the heart of a person at such a time, but that God will grant him what he hopes for and shelters him from what he fears."' [al-Tirmidhi].*

There are a number of issues of importance relating to just after death; what is done when a person dies in terms of washing the body, performing the funeral prayer and burial. There are also issues of importance relating to what actions can benefit the person after their death.

2. Before death

2.1 The one imminently approaching death [*al-muhtadar*]

A person approaching death *[referred to as al-muhtadar]* should be made to lie on his or her right side facing towards the *qiblah* just as one is laid in the grave. This tradition has been passed down from generation to generation within the Muslim community.

> *"Abu Qatadah relates 'Upon arrival in Madinah, the Prophet* 🌸 *enquired about al-Bara ibn Ma'rur. The Prophet was told that he had died, and bequeathed one third of his property be given to the Prophet* 🌸 *and that his face be turned toward the Ka'bah at his death. When the Prophet* 🌸 *heard this he praised him.'" [al-Hakim, Mustadrak, 1:505].*

2.2 Encouragement to say the Testification of Faith [*al-Talqin*]

> *'Umar used to say "Remain close to your dying people, encouraging them to recite 'La illaha illallah, close their eyes and recite the Qur'an next to them" [Abdul Razaq, Al-Musanaf, v3, pg 386].*

When a person is nearing death the Prophet 🌸 ordered that others perform what is termed *talqin* - to gently encourage the dying person to say the testification of faith. He 🌸 said *"Whoever's last words are 'There is no god but God, will enter Paradise." [Abu Dawud, 3116].*

2.2.1 Is *Talqin* only done while the person is alive?

The tradition related to reciting and encouraging people during death to recite the testification of faith are literally addressed to the person who is dead, meaning that this should be done after a persons soul has left their body. However, scholars differ whether the hadith is literal or if it refers to a person close to death before their soul has departed. Commenting on this Imam al-Sharunbulali says:

> *"Performing talqin after the person is placed within the grave is allowed (mashru') on account of the literal meaning of [the hadith] 'Gently encourage (talqin) your dead to say the testification of faith' which is related by 'The Group' except for al-Bukhari, a position that is ascribed to the Ahl as-Sunnah.*
>
> *It is said that this should not be done while the deceased is in the grave, which is the position that is ascribed to the Mu'tazilah. It is also said that this should neither be encouraged or discouraged.*
>
> *The manner of performing this is to say 'O so and so! Remember your faith which you adhered to while on this Earth, testifying that there is no god but God and that Mohammed is His Messenger!' It is clear that words are not taken out of their literal meanings except on account of a binding proof [indicating otherwise]. Therefore it is more apt that what is intended by the words "Your dead" is the literal meaning"* [Maraqih al-Falah, pg324-325].

Similarly, the prominent Hanafi jurist Ibn Humam, in his commentary of the text book al-Hidayah, states that there is no reason to deviate from the literal reading of the hadith which states *'Encourage your dead people to pronounce 'There is no god but God'* as the dead can still hear the living and act accordingly. He takes as his proof the hadith related by Imam Muslim *"Indeed the deceased hears the shuffling of their sandals when they are leaving..."* [§ 2870].

3. Immediately after death

It is an established custom to close the eyes of the deceased after their soul has been taken by the angel of death. When the Prophet ﷺ visited Abu Salamah he closed his eyes saying, *"When a soul is taken the eyes should follow."* [Muslim] 'Umar is reported to have instructed his son with something similar.

> *Bakr ibn Abdillah al-Muzani said 'When you close the eyes of the dead say 'Bismillah wa alla millati Rasullilah (In the name of God and true to the community of the Prophet of God ﷺ). Then he said 'Subhanallah!' and recited the verse "and the angels sing the praises of their Lord [42:5]."* [al-Qurtubi, al-Tadhkirah, pg 39].

3.1 Mourning

The recommendation to observe patience is advice that is given for all calamities and tribulations, but none more so than when dealing with the death of a loved one.

It is related that the Prophet ﷺ passed by a woman who was crying next to a grave and he said to her *"Be aware of God and hold fast to patience"* [Al-Bukhari]. One is recommended to remember God and to supplicate with words taught by the Messenger ﷺ.

> *Umm Salamah said 'The Prophet ﷺ stated 'If a servant of God is afflicted with a tribulation and says 'Truly to God we belong and to Him we shall return, O God reward me in this trouble of mine and provide me in its place that which is better,' God will accept the prayer, providing a reward for their tribulation replacing it with something better. Umm Salamah said 'When my husband died I invoked God using the words taught to me by the Prophet ﷺ and God did grant me someone that was better than him.'"* [Muslim]

It is strongly reprehensible to practice excessive wailing and mourning for one who passes away as it is a sign of one's displeasure of the Divine decree. It is because of this that the Messenger of God ﷺ is reported by Umm Atiyyah to have made the women of the Ansar pledge an oath that *'they would not wail over their dead.'* [Al-Bukhari]

Expressing genuine grief and shedding tears is a sign of the mercy of God. The Prophet ﷺ said upon the death of his son Ibrahim, *"The eyes shed tears and the heart is saddened but we only utter that which pleases our Lord. O Ibrahim! How grieved we are at your departure."* [Al-Bukhari].

Upon being asked by Sa'd ibn Ubadah as to why he was crying on death of his granddaughter Umamah, the daughter of Zaynab, the Prophet ﷺ said *'This is mercy that God has placed within the hearts of his servants, indeed God bestows mercy upon those that are merciful to His servants.'*

3.2 Offering condolences [Ta'ziyyah]

Condolences may be given before as well as after the funeral prayer and burial. The Messenger ﷺ said, *"He who consoles the one in distress shall be rewarded as much as the bereaved."* [al-Tirmidhi]. The Prophet ﷺ would make it a point to visit the families of those that lost loved ones and recommended others to do so. It is related that he would say, *"Indeed to God belongs what he has taken and to Him belongs that which He has given. All things have a set appointed time."* [al-Bukhari].

Imam al-Bukhari entitled one of the chapters in his hadith collection *'Chapter: Whoever sits after a bereavement does so in a way that the signs of sorrow are apparent on them'* in which he mentioned the hadith of Aishah when she said, *"At the instance of the martyrdom of Zayd ibn Harithah, Jafar and Abdullah ibn Rawahah, the Prophet ﷺ sat in the Masjid and the signs of sadness were plain to see"* [1299]. Ibn Hajr said commenting on the title that Imam Bukhari gave to the chapter:

> *"Al-Zayn ibn Munir said "The fiqh in this chapter heading is that the preferred path in all things is best, so if a person is afflicted by a major calamity they should not be excessive in their grief to the point that it leads to prohibited practices such as slapping oneself, tearing at one's clothes and wailing. However they should also not go to the other extreme and be cold and distant such that it diminishes the nature of the affliction. They should follow the Prophet ﷺ in such states, sit for a certain period of time displaying solemnness (waqar) and tranquility (sakinah) with a demeanor of sadness that gives an indication that the calamity that has befallen them is indeed great."* [Ibn Hajr, Fath al-Bari, v3, pg 231].

3.2.1 Offering condolences to those of other faiths

Similarly one should extend one's condolences to the family of whoever dies, enjoining them to show patience and fortitude through their difficulty and that it be a means for them to reflect on the purpose of life.

> *"It is related from [Imam] Malik that a person should extend condolences to his or her non-Muslim neighbour upon the death of a parent because of the responsibility imposed through being neighbours, and if he meets him he should say 'I have heard of the calamity that has befallen you regarding your father. May God give him a place amongst the most revered of his religion and the best of his community!' Sahnun mentioned that he should say 'May God make easy your calamity, and grant you a reward greater than that granted to anyone of your religion."* [Ibn Rushd al-Jidd, al-Bayan wal-Tahsil, v2 pg 212].

3.3 Donating acts of charity, devotion and supplication to the dead.

3.3.1 One's own actions

Once a person has passed away, all of their actions come to an end and their ability to gain reward finishes except by means of the ongoing benefit of good actions they did when on earth. The Prophet ﷺ said *"When a person dies all of actions come to an end except for three: An ongoing charity; knowledge by which benefit is had and pious offspring that pray for him."* [Muslim, 4223].

Various prophetic traditions mention other actions that perpetually give benefit after death. Abu Hurayrah said that the Messenger ﷺ said, *"From the things that reach a person of his actions and good deeds is: knowledge that he has spread; pious offspring he has left behind; a mushaf that he has passed down; a masjid he has built; a rest-house for wayfarers he has constructed; a stream he has excavated and charity that he gave from his wealth while alive and well. [This] reaches him after his death"* [Ibn Majah, 242].

3.3.2 Actions of others on behalf of the dead

The Ahl al-Sunnah, as clearly stated in the earliest creed books such as that of Imam al-Tahawi, hold that the dead gain benefit from the actions of the living. Some, following the lead of the now defunct Mu'tazilah, deny that a dead person can gain any benefit from other actions, misunderstanding the verse of Qur'an *"that no soul shall carry the burden of another and that man will only have that what they have earned for themselves"* [53:38-9]. This logic is rejected by scholars based on the actions of both the early Muslims (*salaf*) as well as those that came after them (*khalaf*). As the hadith master Ibn Salah states:

"...The verse of the Quran mentioned does not show that the opinion that such reward reaches the dead is wrong. The purpose of the verse [is to explain] that the deceased has no right to and no recompense for anything except for what he himself has actually done. Crucially, this does not include what others may do for him; be it an act of charity, the recitation of Quran or supplication" [Ibn Salah, al-Fatawa, 1:149].

The majority of scholars say this includes acts such as monetary charity; the payment of debts; performance of Hajj; *du'a* and supplications as well as the recitation of Qur'an and *dhikr*.

"The rule of thumb in this issue is that a person may donate the reward of any action he or she does to someone else, be it prayer, fasting, charity or anything else. This is according to the Ahl al-Sunnah wal Jamah who base it on the fact that the Prophet ﷺ sacrificed two large sheep, one on behalf of himself while the other was on behalf of all those of his nation who attested to the oneness of God and gave testimony to him ﷺ having conveyed the message." [al-Mirghinani, Hidayah, 1:183].

3.3.2.1 Reciting the Qur'an for the deceased

"The companion Ma'qal ibn Yasar relates that the Prophet ﷺ said "Sura Yasin is the heart of the Qur'an. None recites it seeking the pleasure of God in the hereafter except that they will be forgiven, so recite it upon your dead." [Ahmed, v5, pg 661].

Imam al-Sha'bi said "If one of the Ansar passed away, people would visit the grave at different times to recite Quran there." [Ibn Qayyim al-Jawziyyah, Kitab al-Ruh, pg 37].

Muhammed al-Mirwazi said that he heard Imam Ahmed ibn Hanbal say "Whenever you enter the cemetery recite the Fatiha as well as the Mu'awwadhatayn together with "Qul huwa Allahu Ahad" and confer the reward of this to those inhabiting the graves, for it will surely reach them." [al-Qurtabi, al-Tadhkirah, pg 81; al-Mirdawi al-Hanbali, al-Insaf, v1, pg 412-3].

One of the most widespread practices in the Muslim world amongst scholars and lay people alike is the recitation of the Qur'an with the intention of presenting the reward of the action to the deceased. However some people, who may sometimes be otherwise lax in their religious practice, insist that such recitation is an essential part of the rituals of death. Others have made this into a matter of creed and faith, condemning the custom of gathering to reciting the Qur'an and questioning the faith of those that attend such gatherings.

The truth is that while there may be some recognized difference amongst scholars on this issue, it never reached the level where one group attacked the other. As is was well known amongst scholars *"A practice on which there is an accepted disagreement is not to be condemned. What is condemned is only that upon which there is an agreement as to it being prohibited"*

There are some scholars from the Shafi'i and Maliki schools that differentiate between reciting at the graveside, which they permit, and reciting the Qur'an from far, which they deem not to benefit the dead. The majority of scholars however state that just as supplications and du'a reach the deceased whether it is done from near or far, so too is the case of reciting the Qur'an. Hence the Ahl al-Sunnah agree on the permissibility of reciting near the grave, but differ on it being done away from the grave.

Qadi 'Iyad al Maliki in his commentary on the hadith of the two fresh branches in which the Prophet ﷺ said *"They may well lighten their ordeal as long as they do not wilt"* says *"Scholars take from this the recommendation to recite the Qur'an for the deceased, because if a person's punishment is lightened through the glorification (tasbih) of two branches, which are after all inanimate, then more so the recitation of the Qur'an...!"*

As for the Hanbali school, it holds that all types of actions done for the dead, whether from near or far, are of benefit to them.

*'**Any type of good deed**' be it supplication, istigh'far, prayer, fasting, hajj or reciting the Qur'an as well as other actions '**the reward of which are donated to the dead, benefit them**'. Imam Ahmed said 'All types of good action reach the dead' based on the relevant sacred text on this subject. Muslims have congregated in all places reciting Qur'an and presenting (the reward) to their dead without any one objecting so that it a matter of consensus (ijma') just like supplication and istighfar. So much so that if it was presented to the*

Prophet ﷺ this would be permitted and the reward would reach him ﷺ as is mentioned by al-Majd[12]" [Ibn Muflih, al-Mubdi', v2, 279].

---

[12] *Majd al-Din, Abd al-Salam ibn 'Abdillah (d. 652h). The author of al-Muntaqa in hadith al-Ahkam; al-Maswada in Usul; al-Muharir in Fiqh. He is also the grand father of Ibn Taymiyyah.*

Lesson 5
The funeral prayer and burial

Lesson Five
Aim: To be able to understand the theory and practice of conducting the funeral prayer.

Objectives:
Having successfully completed this lesson, students should be able to demonstrate the ability to:
1. **Explain** the rulings related to the funeral prayer including the prerequisites and conditions of the prayer.
2. **Outline** how a dead person is washed and shrouded
3. **Summarize** the method of performing the funeral prayer.
4. **Detail** how a person is buried.
5. **Outline** the ruling of the etiquette of visiting graves.

---

1. The meaning of *Janazah*

Janazah literally means *'to cover over'* and something that hangs heavy on a people over which there is great sadness is also termed a *janazah*. As the poet says:

> *'I never feared that I would become a burden of sorrows (janazah)*
> *upon your shoulders - and who is it that is so deceived by events?'*[13]

2. The funeral prayer

2.1 Ruling. The funeral prayer is a communal obligation (*fard kifayah*) and so the obligation of performing it is lifted from the whole community only when it is properly undertaken by some of them.

2.2 The prerequisites of the funeral prayer

Ritual purity, as with all other types of prayer, is a precondition for the offering of the funeral prayer. This means that one should be free of both major and minor impurity before offering the funeral prayer. Abdullah ibn 'Umar used to say, *"One should not pray a funeral prayer unless one is in a state of ritual purity."* [Imam Malik, al-Muwatta]. [14]

2.3 Conditions of the funeral prayer

2.3.1 The deceased being a Muslim.

Since the funeral prayer is a type of worship which is a right that a muslim deceased has over the whole community, it is only performed for those that have accepted the salvific nature of such a prayer through entering into the Muslim faith. *"And never pray upon any one of them who dies neither stand upon their grave for indeed they disbelieved in God and his Messenger and died in a state of transgression."* [9:84].

2.3.2 Being washed before the prayer is performed.

2.3.2.1 Washing the dead body

The Prophet ﷺ said *"A Muslim has six rights over other Muslims"* [Muslim] and mentioned washing the deceased as one of them. Every Muslim that has passed away should be washed and shrouded before the funeral prayer is performed.

2.3.2.2 Who should perform the washing

---

[13] *Ibn Faris, Maqa'is al-Lughah, v1, 485*

[14] If one thinks that attaining purity will lead to missing a funeral prayer which is about to take place then one is permitted to perform *tayammum* in such circumstances. This dispensation is not extended to other prayers since they can be made up later, however the funeral prayer cannot be made up once it is missed.

The general ruling is that men should be washed by men and women should be washed by women. However, it is allowed for a woman to wash the body of her dead husband. It is also recommended that the family themselves perform the washing.

2.3.2.3 The method of washing the deceased

The body should be washed at least once, although it is recommended that this be done three times.
- Clothing should be removed and a piece of cloth placed upon the deceased covering their nakedness (*awra*).
- Gentle pressure should be applied to the stomach area to remove any impurities which should be then be washed away.
- The one carrying out the washing should cover their hands with suitable gloves or a cloth while washing the private parts of the deceased.
- The limbs that are washed in wudu should then be cleaned in the same order as one would perform wudu. The Prophet ﷺ said *"Begin by washing the deceased from the right side of the body, washing those parts that are washed during wudu."* [Al-Bukhari].
- One should lay the body on its left side allowing one to wash the right part of the body thoroughly, a process that should be repeated for the other side using water and soap.
- One then makes the deceased sit up and cleans any dirt that comes out of the bodily passages.
- If it is felt that three washes are not enough to properly clean the body then this may be increased by an odd number. The Prophet ﷺ said *"Wash the deceased an odd number of times namely three, five or seven"* [Al-Bukhari].
- If any impurities come out of the body during washing then only the impurities need to be washed and one does not need to repeat either the ghusl or the wudu.

2.3.2.4 Drying and preparing the washed body

It is recommended that the body be dried after the washing process and that it be perfumed as well. Umm Attiyah said *"The Prophet ﷺ came out when one of his daughters had died and said 'Wash her three, five or more times if you consider it necessary using water and lote tree leaves and upon finishing the last washing, apply some camphor to the body. Once you have done this let me know.' Once we had done this we informed him ﷺ. He ﷺ gave us a cloth from around his waist ﷺ and said "Wrap her first in this."* [Al-Bukhari, 1258]

One should not cut the hair, shave or otherwise groom the deceased.

2.3.3 The shroud.

The Prophet ﷺ said, *"Wear white clothes, for these are your best clothes, and shroud your dead in them."* [Ibn Majah].

The costs of the burial and shroud should be taken directly from the estate of the deceased. This is the first right on what has been left behind before such things as the distribution of inheritance and any Will (*wasiyyah*) left. If there is no money from which the costs can be settled it is a communal obligation that the funeral expenses be met to cover the burial.

2.3.3.1 *The shroud of the male*

Scholars agree that for the male, the shroud consists of three plain sheets. In this regard it is related on the authority of Aishah that she said, *"The Messenger of God ﷺ was wrapped in three pieces of white cloth from Yemen without a (sewn) shirt or turban."* [Al-Bukhari].

It is only allowed to use less than this if nothing else is available.

The three pieces are: (1) An outer sheet (*lifaf*); (2) A loin cloth (*izar*); (3) Shirt (*qamis*).

2.3.3.2 *The shroud of the female*

This is made up of five sheets of cloth; (1) an outer sheet (*lifaf*); (2) A loin cloth (*izar*); (3) Shirt (*qamis*); (4) Chest wrap (*khirqah*); (5) Scarf (*khimar*).

Before the shroud has been closed, it is recommended that one rub perfume and camphor upon the parts of the body that touch the ground during prostration.

2.3.4 The deceased being physically present and placed in front of the congregation

This means that the majority of the body of the deceased be present in front of the Imam leading the prayer. It is therefore not permitted to pray a funeral prayer upon a person who is not physically present in front of the congregation. However there is a scholarly difference of opinion on this issue. Some scholars do allow the funeral prayer on a body that is not present.

It is related that the Prophet ﷺ lead the funeral prayer for the Ethiopian ruler *Najashi*. However it is considered to be amongst the peculiar qualities *(khasa'is)* and miracles of the Prophet ﷺ and it is related that the distance between Madinah and Ethiopia became insignificant for him ﷺ in the same way that Masjid al-'Aqsa was shown to him ﷺ when the Quraysh mocked the Muslims regarding his night journey to Jerusalem. *[al-Mazari, Mu'lim fi Sharh Muslim,1/488].*

'Imran ibn Hussain related that the Prophet ﷺ stood to perform the funeral prayer on *Najashi* and the people made rows behind him. None of them thought anything except that the body was in front of them. *"We prayed behind him and we didn't think anything other than that the body was in front of us" [Ibn Hajar, Fath Al-Bari, v3 188].* Many of the Prophet's ﷺ Companions died in distant lands, but it is not related in the Prophet ﷺ ever prayed the funeral prayer for anyone who was not physically present. *[al-Qarafi, adh-Dhakhirah,1/136].*

2.3.5 The intention to pray to God and supplicate for the deceased

3. The actions of the funeral prayer

3.1 Pillars (*Arkan*)
    3.1.1 Performing the prayer standing.
    3.1.2 Four *takbir*

3.2 Obligatory (*wajib*)
    3.2.1 The *Salam* at the end of the prayer.

3.3 Sunnan
    3.3.1 That the Imam stand next to the chest of the deceased;
    3.3.2 Reciting *"al-Thana"* after the first takbir;
    3.3.3 Invoking prayers upon the Prophet ﷺ after the second *takbir*;
    3.3.4 Supplicating for the deceased after the third takbir.

4. How to perform the Funeral Prayer

4.1 The first Takbir.
Both the imam and the congregation raise their hands at the first takbir. For the rest of the *takbirs*, the congregation do not raise their hands.
After the Imam has initiated the prayer, one reads the supplication recommended in the first *rak'ah* of a usual prayer. The *Fatihah* may also be read at his point, but with the intention of it being a supplication for the deceased.

4.2 The second takbir
After the second *takbir* one should recite the prayer on the Prophet ﷺ.

4.3 The third Takbir
The funeral supplication for the deceased is recited after the third *takbir*. There are a number of narrated supplications in this regard.

اللَّهُمَّ اغْفِرْ لَهُ وَارْحَمْهُ وَعَافِهِ وَاعْفُ عَنْهُ , وَأَكْرِمْ نُزُلَهُ وَوَسِّعْ مُدْخَلَهُ وَاغْسِلْهُ بِالْمَاءِ وَالثَّلْجِ وَالْبَرَدِ وَنَقِّهِ مِنْ الْخَطَايَا كَمَا يُنَقَّى الثَّوْبُ الْأَبْيَضُ مِنْ الدَّنَسِ , وَأَبْدِلْهُ دَارًا خَيْرًا مِنْ دَارِهِ وَأَهْلًا خَيْرًا مِنْ أَهْلِهِ وَزَوْجًا خَيْرًا مِنْ زَوْجِهِ , وَأَدْخِلْهُ الْجَنَّةَ وَأَعِذْهُ مِنْ عَذَابِ الْقَبْرِ وَعَذَابِ النَّارِ

"O God! Forgive him, have mercy on him, pardon him, heal him, be generous to him, cause his entrance to be wide and comfortable, wash him with the most pure and clean water, and purify him from sins as a white garment is washed clean of dirt. Give him in exchange a home better than his home (on earth) and a family better than his family, and a spouse better than his spouse, and protect him from the trial of the grave and the torture of Hell Fire" [Muslim].

4.4 The fourth Takbir

This is the last *takbir* after which the *salam* is given to the right and left.[15]

Notes:
- The one with the most right to lead the prayer is the resident Imam, then the next of kin of the deceased.
- A person that has committed suicide is washed and prayed upon.
- Stillborn children are washed, placed in a cloth and buried, however there is no funeral prayer for still born children. In the case of miscarriage, the fetus, if the limbs are formed, is treated as a stillborn.
- A child that showed signs of life after being born is treated like any other dead person so is named, given a *ghusl*, shrouded after which the funeral prayer is performed.

5. Burial

The burial should be done immediately once the funeral prayer has been performed. The body should be placed with the head facing towards the direction of Mecca. It is recommended that one say the following *du'a* when lowering the deceased into the grave: *"In the Name of God and upon the community of the Messenger of God ﷺ.'* It is recommended that those present place soil from the side of the grave into the grave three times. During the first handful one should recite *'and from the earth did we create you'*, during the second and *'into it we will return you'* and when placing the third handful one should say *'and from it we shall bring you to life once again.'*

6. Visiting the graveyard

> The Prophet ﷺ said *"Visit graveyards for surely it will remind you of death and the Hereafter."* [Muslim]. It is also related that he ﷺ said, *"Whoever visits the grave of their parents every Friday will be granted forgiveness and will be recorded as an obedient child of their parents."* [al-Bayhaqi].

Aishah reports that she asked the Messenger ﷺ *"What should I say when I pass through a graveyard O Messenger of God ﷺ?'* He replied *'Say 'Peace be upon the believing men and women dwelling here! May God grant mercy to those that have preceded us and those that are to follow for, God willing, we will indeed join you.'"* [Muslim].

This is a recommendation that includes both men and women, though women who are unable to control their emotions leading them to excessive wailing and mourning are discouraged from going.

Al-Hakim relates that Abdullah ibn Abi Mulaykah narrates that he asked Aishah after her having visited the graveyard *'O Mother of the Believers, where have you been?'* She said *'I went out to visit the grave of my brother Abd al-Rahman'.* *'Did the Messenger ﷺ not prohibit visiting graves?'* I said. She replied *'Yes, he had forbidden the visitation of the graveyard earlier, but later on he ordered us to visit them.'"* [al-Hakim].

6.1 Reciting Qur'an at the graveside

> *"It is narrated that Imam Ahmed censured a blind man from reciting at a grave saying, "Reciting at the grave is a blameworthy innovation (bid'ah)." Muhammad ibn Qudama al-Jawhari said to the him, "Abu 'Abdullah! What is your opinion of Mubshir al-Halabi?" He replied, "Why he is both trustworthy and reliable (thiqah)!" Al-Jawhari then replied, "Mubshir narrated to me that his father left a will stipulating that when he died the opening and closing verses of surah al-Baqarah should be read after he has been buried.*
>
> *He then said, 'I heard Ibn 'Umar state this in his will also.[16]'" Imam Ahmad ibn Hanbal said, "Go back and tell that man to go ahead and recite" [Ibn Qayyim, Kitab al-Ruh, pg 37; Ibn Qudamah, Al-Mughni, vol. 2, pg. 224; Imam al-Mirdawi, al-Insaf, v1, pg 412].*

---

[15] If one who joins the prayer late, they should wait for the next *takbir* of the Imam at which point one should join the prayer. If one is aware of how many *takbir* have been missed, they should partake in reciting what the imam is reciting, otherwise one acts according to one's strongest inclination. When the Imam finishes, one performs the missed *takbir*.[al-Shurunbulali, Maraqih]

[16] See al-Bayhaqi, Sunan al-Kubra, v4, pg 56. al-Hafidh ibn Hajar in his work Amali al-Adhkar classified this narration from Ibn 'Umar as 'mawquf hasan'.

Lesson 6
In the shade of *"Every innovation is a misguidance"*

> **Aim: Lesson six:** To understand the issues related to the concept of innovation in Islamic law and theology.
>
> **Objectives:**
> Having successfully completed this lesson, students should be able to demonstrate the ability to:
> 1. **Outline** the nature of the discussion and why it is important to place the issue in the proper context.
> 2. **Mention** the two types of prophetic traditions that make mention of innovation and how they are understood.
> 3. **Summarize** what is meant by the phrase *'Every innovation'* in the light of what has been said regarding this by scholars.
> 4. **Mention and explain** a definition of Innovation arrived at by scholars with particular emphasis on how to differentiate between the various types of innovation.
> 5. **List** the three conditions for a practice to be deemed a *'good innovation'*.
> 6. **Summarize** the points made by those that say that *'Every innovation...'* is to be taken literally and how the majority have responded to these points.

> *"Innovation is of two types: Innovation of guidance and that of misguidance. Whatever runs counter to the command of God and His Messenger* ﷺ *is within the sphere of blame and condemnation. Whatever enters into the generality of what God or His Prophet* ﷺ *recommended or stressed is praiseworthy [...]. It is in this sense that the hadith "Every innovation is misguidance" is understood. [It means] whatever contravenes the bases of the Law and is not in harmony with the Sunna..."* [Ibn Athir, al-Nihayah fi Garib al-Hadith, V1, 112-113].

An issue that has increasingly been given prominence in recent times amongst Muslims is the concept of innovation (*Bid'ah*), so much so that some have insisted on turning it into an issue of *Aqidah* (Creed) and one of the core issues upon which a person's religious practice should be assessed. We all hear people casually dismissing practices as being *'Shirk'* or *'Bid'ah'* without any real appreciation of what they are saying. Indeed if it were not for the recent trend of conflating such issues as part of Creed, there would be little need for the present discussion. How then can we reach a balanced understanding of what the word *Bid'ah* means?

1. Placing the discussion on *Bid'ah* in the proper context
-Authenticity (*thubut*) and meaning (*dalalah*)

1.1 The first thing to notice in this issue is that the hadith texts that mention the condemnation of what is translated as *'innovation'* are not mutawatir, but solitary narrations that are *Dhanni al-Thabut*. As opposed to the many religious matters that are known to be integral to Islamic faith and practice, the issue of innovation is certainly not of the type which could justify making it the basis of condemning others. As we shall see, the majority of renowned Islamic scholars of the past had a far from polarized understanding of this question.

1.2 The other issue which needs to be addressed is that of the meaning of the hadith (*dalalah*). Are they to be taken to have only their literal meaning or are they open to interpretation? To answer this question we will need to look at the wording of the hadith themselves.

2. Prophetic traditions on Innovation

The origin of this discussion is rooted in a number of hadith that speak of *'newly invented matters'*. There are two types of Prophetic traditions related to innovations.

2.1 Absolute Hadith

The first of these have wording that is absolute in meaning, implying the condemnation of every innovation.

> Jabir ibn Abdullah relates that the Prophet ﷺ said *"Indeed the best of speech is the Book of God and the best of guidance is the guidance of Muhammed. The worst acts are those that*

are newly invented and every (kullu) innovation is leading astray." [Muslim 867, Ahmed v3 pg310].

2.2 Qualified Hadith

The second are Prophetic traditions which qualify innovations as being of different types which implies innovations having different rulings.

> "Whoever innovates an innovation of misguidance which is not pleasing to God and His Messenger will have the sin of whoever acts in accordance with it without it decreasing the sin of people in any way." [al-Tirmidhi].

> Aishah relates that the Prophet ﷺ said 'Whoever brings into being (ahdatha) an act in this matter of ours that is not of it will have it rejected.' [al-Bukhari, 2697; Muslim, 1718].

2.3 Ground rules for understanding the Hadith

> "This is a general statement which has been specified. What is intended by the words are most innovations." [Imam Nawawi, Sharh Muslim, v6, pg 393].

2.3.1 Reconciliation [17] [Jam']

It is an agreed principle in Islamic jurisprudence that if there are two texts on the same topic, one of which is general and the other specific, then the general is understood in light of the specific text. This is one of the many methods outlined in books of Islamic juristic methodology (*Usul*) to reconcile (*jam'*) between competing texts.

The specific hadith are important in understanding the general, since the Prophet ﷺ used phrases such as:

> '...an innovation **of misguidance which is not pleasing to God and his Messenger**'

implying that some innovations are not misguidance, rather they are pleasing to God and His Messenger ﷺ.

Similarly he ﷺ said:

> '**...that is not of it**'

implying that there are innovations '*that are part*' of the *shari'ah* and in line with divine wisdom and principles. What we see from this second type of hadith is that just as there are innovations that are blameworthy, so too there are innovations that are praiseworthy, all depending on how close these practices are to the legal principles of the *shari'ah*. That innovations can be both good and bad is further illustrated in the hadith of Jarir ibn 'Abdillah al-Bajali in which he narrates that the Prophet ﷺ said:

> "Whoever brings a good practice into being (sanna) in Islam will have its reward and the reward of all those who practice it until the Day of Judgement without lessening the rewards of the latter in any way. [Similarly] whoever brings a bad practice into being (sana) in Islam will bear its sin and the sin of all those who practice it until the Day of Judgment without lessening the sin of the latter in any way." [Muslim, 1017]

Conclusion: The meaning of the first Hadith '*Every innovation is misguided*' is understood as referring to blameworthy innovations and not all innovations. The blameworthy nature of a practice is understood from a lack of proof in the *Shari'ah* pointing to it generally being a recommended act.

3. Language - The meaning of 'Every' (kull)

Key to the discussion on *bid'ah* is how to understand the word '*every*' in the hadith of Jabir. Surely it has to mean '*each and every*' innovation as is the literal translation. Is this wording what scholars would refer to as *Qati Al-Dalalah* meaning a phrase or word which has only one possible meaning or is it interpreted in another way?

---

[17] See prayer module 2 lesson 4 for an explanation of this principle.

We know from religious text such as the Qur'an and Sunnah that the word *'every'* is mostly used to mean not *'every'* but *'most or many'*[18]. Just a few examples from the Qur'an show this to be the case.

> **"And proclaim among men the Pilgrimage, and they shall come to you on foot and upon every lean beast, they shall come from every deep ravine...[22:27]**

> *"The word 'every' (kull) is used here to indicate a large number, meaning that they will be on many mounts. Though the word 'kull' in terms of its original donation and meaning refers to the complete inclusion of the whole genus that is appendixes to it [19], it is used in many instances to give the meaning of 'many' such as the verse '...a woman ruling over them who has been given everything' meaning most of the things that are given to those upon the throne[...]. This type of usage occurs three times in the words of [the poet] 'Antarah [Ibn Shaddād al-'Absī][20]:*

>> *'The first pure showers of **every** rain-laden cloud fell upon it,*
>>> *leaving **every** puddle therein shining and emboldened like a silver coin;*
>> *Sprinkling and pouring down; so that the water flows upon it*
>>> ***every** evening such that it is never cut off from it'[21]*

> *This [meaning of 'every'] has already been explained in the verse "And yet, even if you were to place every evidence before those who have been given earlier revelation, they would not follow your direction of prayer...' [2:145] in the Chapter of the Cow."*
> *[Imam Ibn 'Ashur, Tafsir al-Tahrir wal-Tanwir, v7, pg 244].*

Similarly God says about His punishment to a previous nation *"...It will destroy **everything** by the command of its Lord and then in the morning they will see nothing but the ruins of their houses and in this way do we recompense those that transgress."[46:25]* Even though the word *'kull'* is used within this verse, we know that not everything was destroyed, but only their habitations since the mountains, earth and all other creation remained.

In the story of Sulayman (a.s.) and the Queen of Sheba, the hoopoe went and visited the Queen of Sheba and described her and her dominion in the following way *"I have traversed a place that you have not and I have come to you from Saba' with glad tidings. I found there a woman ruling over them who has been given **everything** and she has been endowed with a magnificent throne.'* It is understood that she was not given all things but rather this is a figure of speech meaning that she was given all that they could imagine a monarch to have.

3.1 Conclusion on the meaning of 'every'

Imam Nawawi summarizes the meaning of the hadith *'Every innovation is misguidance'* saying *'This is a general statement which has been specified (al-'amm al-makhsus). What is intended by the words are **most** innovations." [Imam Nawawi, Sharh Muslim, v6, pg 393]*

This is a simple point of Usul that any trained student of knowledge is able to grasp without any difficulty, since it relates to the basic rules of the Arabic language and rhetoric (*balagha*). The words of Imam al-Nawawi go to the crux of the matter and failure to understand this simple point means that the vast majority

---

[18] The finest and most comprehensive book on *Usul* ever written entitled *'The Encompassing Ocean'* mentions the following:
"A point of interest: The vast majority of general statements of the Quran have been specified. So much so that 'Ilm al-Din al-Iraqi stated that only following verses [of Quran] have no exception: (1) "Forbidden to you are your mothers" [4:23]; (2) "All that lives on earth or in the heavens is bound to pass away" [55:26]; (3) 'and God has full knowledge of everything" [2:282]; (4) "and because He has the power to will anything" [22:6]; and (5) "And there is no living creature on earth but depends for its sustenance on God" [11:6]" [al-Zarqashi, al-Bahr al-Muhit. v3, pg 248; al-Shawkani, Irshad al-Fuhul, pg 482].

From this we have the statement ascribed to Imam al-Shafi'i *"There is no general statement that exist except that it has been specified, and if has not already been specified, then it is open to being specified" [Husam al-Din al-Ikhsakiti, al-Mudh'hib fi Usul al-Madh'hab, v1, pg 60].*

[19] *See Ibn Hisham, Mughni al-Labib, v3, pg 84.*

[20] The famous pre-Islamic poet whose poem was attached to the Ka'ba in view of its purity and elegance. He was also an accomplished warrior and his poem dwells on the themes of love and heroism.

[21] *Diwan 'Antara, Dar al-Sadir, pg 18-19.*

of attacks on the majority position, are based on the usual superficiality that has unfortunately marked contemporary Muslim discourse. All because those not qualified in religious scholarship take the reigns of scholarly leadership in the age of a viral mass media.

4. *Definitions of Bidah*

...al-Shafi'i said 'Newly invented matters are of two types; Firstly, those which are innovated and which contradicts a verse of Qur'an; a Prophetic Sunnah; a narration (of a companion) or else consensus. These types are considered innovations of misguidance. Then there are those good things which are innovated and which are not opposed by scholars. These types of innovations are not blameworthy...' [al-Bayhaqi, Manaqib al-Shafi'i, pg253].

Based on the preceding discussions and contrary to modern discourse, the overwhelming majority of Sunni scholars have defined *bid'ah* as being of at least two types. Below is only a represent sample of definitions which set out the rule and not the exception, regarding the position of the Ahl al-Sunnah.

4.1 Al-Ghazzali

"Bid'ah is of two types: one, which is reprehensible, running counter to an ancient sunnah (sunnah qadimah) and will eventually lead to it being changed. Then there is a good bid'ah which is defined as a practice that is newly introduced [but] based upon a previous precedence (ma ahdatha 'ala mithalin sabiqin)" [Ihya 'Ulum al-Din, v1 pg 276].

4.2 Qadi Abu Bakr ibn al-'Arabi al-Maliki

"Know, may God increase you in knowledge, that newly invented matters are of two types: One which has no origin excpet in personal caprice and acting in accordance with one's own opinion. This type is falsehood without any doubt. Secondly newly invented matters based upon drawing an analogy between two similar things. This is the established sunnah of the Khulafah as well as the distinguished scholars.

A newly invented matter and innovation are not condemned merely because they are called newly invented matters or innovations or the meaning they convey, for God Himself has said "and there does not come to them a reminder from their Lord which is newly invented." Similarly 'Umar said 'What a great innovation this is.' What are blameworthy are those matters which stand in contravention to the Sunnah. Newly invented matters which lead to misguidance stand condemned." [Qadi Abu Bakr ibn al-'Arabi al-Maliki, Commentary on al-Tirmidhi, v10, p147].

4.3 Imam Al-Nawawi

"Bid'ah in religious usage is to invent something that did not exist during the time of the Prophet ﷺ and it is broken down into praiseworthy innovation and blameworthy innovation. The Shaykh and the Imam whose religious authority and standing all agree upon and whose firm-footedness in all types of sciences is acknowledged. Abu Muhammed Abdul Aziz ibn Abd al-Salaam said towards the end of his book 'The Maxims':

4.3.1 [Sub-categories of Bidah]

"Bid'ah is broken down into that which is obligatory, prohibited, recommended, reprehensible and permitted. He said the way to understand this is to weight the innovation in the light of general legal maxims. If it is subsumed under a maxim which entails obligation then it is obligatory and if it is subsumed under a maxim which indicates it being prohibited then it is prohibited and likewise [it may be] recommended, reprehensible or permitted [...].

Imam al-Bayhaqi relates with his chain of narration in the book 'Manaqib al-Shafi'i' that [Imam] al-Shafi'i said 'Newly invented matters are of two types: Firstly, those which are innovated and which contradicts a verse of Qur'an; a Prophetic Sunnah; a narration (of a companion) or else a consensus. These types are considered innovations of misguidance. Then there are those good things which are innovated and which are not opposed by scholars. These types of innovations are not blameworthy'. 'Umar said with regards to the night prayers in the month of Ramadan "What a great innovation it is!" meaning that it is a newly invented matter that did not exist in the past and it does not negate anything that came before it." [al-Nawawi, Tahdhib al-Asma, v 3 pg 20-23].

4.4 Badr al-Din Al-'Ayni al-Hanafi

Imam Badr al-Din Al-'Ayni al-Hanafi says in his commentary on Sahih al-Bukhari:

> *"Innovation in its origin is to come up with an action which did not exist during the time of the Prophet ﷺ. Thereafter, Bid'ah is of two types: If it is subsumed under a general act which is considered as being good in the eyes of the Law then it is a praiseworthy Bid'ah. However, it is subsumed under a general act which is blameworthy in the eyes of the law then it is a blameworthy Bid'ah.' [Al-Ayni, Umdat al Qari, v11:136].*

5. Schools of Law and Bid'ah

How have the schools of law understood the issue of *bid'ah* and is it true to say that the majority of scholars have endorsed and agreed with innovation being categorized based upon its agreement or otherwise with the *Shari'ah* as is outlined above?

The Hanafi, Shafi'i and Maliki schools have overwhelmingly endorsed the understanding that *bid'ah* can be both good and bad. Ibn Al-Hajj mentions in his book al-Madkhal the consensus of the Maliki school on this point *[v2 pg 115]*, as does Abu Shama al-Maqdisi, the teacher of Imam An-Nawawi *[pg 12-13]*. The Hanafi school has also recorded its agreement on this understanding of *Bid'ah*. Ibn Abidin in a number of places reiterates the validity of this classification of *bid'ah [v1, 376]*. Only the position of the Hanbali school, due to the positions of its later scholars, is ambiguous.[22]

6. Conditions of a good innovation

6.1 The matter should be subsumed under an already existing source of the *Shari'ah* or subservient to a central aim enshrined in religious law. An example of this is 'Umar collecting people to pray 20 *rakat* for tarawih as it is not recorded that the Prophet ﷺ ever prayed 20 *rakat*.

6.2 The matter should not contravene a specific religious source-text (*nass*) and that it not lead to the neglect of an established Sunnah. Imam Al-Ghazali says in his definition *"a disliked bid'ah is that which contravenes an ancient sunnah or will eventually lead to it being changed."* An example of this would be to engage in extra acts of worship or *dhikr* to the point that one gives no importance to those enjoined in the prophetic *sunnah*.

6.3 The innovation should be something that the community generally agrees upon after it having already conformed to the previous conditions. Imam al-'Ayni mentions this point whilst speaking about praiseworthy innovation saying *"It is that which the Muslim community deems to be good as long as it does not go against the Book, Sunnah or Consensus."* An example of this is the extra *adhan* instigated during the Khilafah of 'Uthman based upon the need for this due, to the large numbers attending the prayer.

7. Innovations performed by early scholars that where not done by the Prophet ﷺ

There are many instances of the Salaf and Khalaf doing new actions in accordance with the conditions above. Even Ibn Taymiyyah is reported by his own close student al-Hafiz Umar Al-Bazzar to have had the habit of sitting after completing the *Fajr* prayer to recite the Fatiha recurrently until the prohibition from praying passed. It is well known that it is not the Sunnah to repeat the Fatiha during the period of this time and it is not narrated in any Hadith that any of the Salaf used to do so which would class his act as a *bidah*.

Dua at the completion (khatim) of Qur'an

> *Al-Fadl ibn Zayd said "I asked Abu Abdullah about completing the Qur'an. Should I make it coincide with the witr prayer or should it be done in the Tarawih?' He replied: 'Make it coincide with the tarawih so that one can supplicate between the two.' I asked him 'How should*

---

[22] According to the Hanbali scholars Ibn Taymiyyah and Ibn Rajab, the word Bid'ah was used by the *salaf* to convey two different meanings. The first was the use of innovation in a *linguistic sense* to mean something new without precedence as in the words of Umar regarding the Tarawih prayer *"What a great Bid'ah this is"*. This type of usage is according to them acceptable and does not point to the reprehensible nature of the act done. The second use of the word *Bid'ah* is according to them wholly negative and indicates the impermissibility of the act. This type of usage they define as the *legal definition* of innovation as used by the Prophet ﷺ in his words *"Every innovation is misguidance"*. It is worthy to note that if the word had such a negative connotation and if all innovations were really a misguidance then for 'Umar ؓ to use the term *'bidah'* within a positive context would imply that he condoned the ambiguous use of a negative word.

I do this?' He said 'Once you have completed the end of the Qur'an you should raise your hands before bowing and supplicate for us while in prayer standing for a long period.' I asked him 'With what should one supplicate?' He said 'With whatever you wish'. I did as he informed me while he was behind me standing and supplicating with his hands raised. Hanbal said 'I heard Ahmad say concerning completing the Qur'an 'Once you have recited say 'I seek refuge in the Lord of mankind', one should raise one's hands in supplication before one bows down. I asked 'Upon what does he base this?' He replied 'I saw the people of Mecca doing this and Sufyan Ibn 'Uyaynah used to lead them with this practice in Mecca.' [Ibn Qudamah v1 pg. 802].

8. The proofs of those that hold all *bid'ah* as blameworthy.

As mentioned above the vast majority of scholars that have looked into this issue have stated that innovations can be both good and bad and this was the overriding opinion of scholars. However, there have been some renowned Imams who stated that any newly invented matter is to be condemned regardless of the benefit ascribed to it by scholars. They took the position of negating the majority understanding and have insisted that every innovation and newly invented matter is unjustified. Most important of these are the three scholars Ibn Taymiyyah, Imam Al-Shatibi and Ibn Rajab al-Hanbali. Their proofs for their position can be summarized in the following three points:

8.1 *That the religion is complete*. The Qur'an says *"Today I have perfected for you your religion, completed my favor to you and I am well pleased with Islam as a religion for you [5:3]."* Therefore, they argue that anything that is introduced later would imply that the *Shari'ah* was incomplete and so imperfect.

8.1.1 *The response to this* is that this verse means that there will be no subsequent revelation, but does not negate the further development of religious law and practice as long as such developments are in keeping with the teachings of the Qur'an and Sunnah. This understanding of the verse is upheld in the conditions mentioned above for an innovation being acceptable.

8.2 *'Every innovation is misguided.'* It is argued that the Prophet ﷺ never used the word innovation except in a negative context for something opposed to the Sunnah.

8.2.1 *The response to this* by the majority of scholars has already been given extensively above in section 3.

8.3 *The sayings of the Salaf*. We find many narrations from them that condemn innovation without differentiation between different types of innovation. Ibn Abbas said, *"Never did a year pass but that people introduced an innovation in it and caused the death of a Sunnah until innovation was given life and the Sunan died."* [al-Haytami, Majma' al-Zawaid, 1/88].

8.3.1 *This is the most important point made by those that have a strict understanding of bidah and so the response to this* is also the most important for understanding why this issue has become so misunderstood recently.

The early community were generally weary of *all* new issues that arose in the community **even if they later on came to accept them**, such as the need to collect the Qur'an into a single document; setting down the hadith in writing; fighting those that separated between zakat and prayer and so on. Any initial denunciation was to rein in unrestricted appearance of new matters, or things the previous generation did not feel the need to do. This still means that the *salaf* assessed each new matter on its own merit and did not adhere to a position of blanket rejection that has become so prevalent today. Understanding the words of Ibn al-Jawzi al-Hanbali below are pivotal in properly understanding the whole debate on *bidah*. It clarifies the stance of the *Salaf* and resolves any misunderstandings that have occurred in recent times:

"If something was brought into being which did not run contrary to the Shari'ah and did not stand to oppress it, in such situations the majority of the Salaf still used to disapprove of it. They used to dissuade others from all types of innovation even if they were permitted, in order to preserve the original principle which is to follow (ittiba'). In this context Zaid bin Thabit said to Abu Bakr and 'Umar when they asked to him collect the Qur'anic revelation 'How can you both attempt to do something which was not done by the Prophet?'

*Some would warn against all innovations even if there was no inherent problem, just so that people did not bring into being practices that did not exist in the past. **[However], many newly invented matters that neither ran contrary to the Shari'ah, nor opposed it eventually came into being and they did not see any problem with them**, such as 'Umar collecting people together to stand during Ramadan and when he saw them he said, 'What a great innovation this is.' [Ibn Jawzi, Talbis al-Iblis, pg8].*

Endnote on the true concept of Innovation

It should be pointed out that the use of the word *bid'ah* in the early community was used almost exclusively for innovations in areas of Creed (*aqidah*). Even a cursory review of books of biographical works show that the term *"People of Innovation"* was used for those that held to erroneous and misguided beliefs regarding God and His Attributes, Free will and Predestination *(Qada and Qadar)* and the status of a person who commits major sins etc. Therefore this word was used to describe groups such as the Khawarij, Mu'tazillah, Qadariyyah and so on.

> *"The erudite scholars of the Maturidi and 'Ashari [schools of theology] do not accuse one another of innovation and misguidance as opposed to those that are extreme and fanatical, who may go to such an extent as to take a difference of opinion in secondary matters to be tantamount to innovation and misguidance...*
>
> *Such individuals fail to understand that a reprehensible innovation is something which is innovated in religious matters which did not exist during the time of the Companions or those that followed them and furthermore does not have a supporting basis in the Shari'ah. Amongst these ignorant ones are those that take any matter which did not exist at the time of the Companions to be a reprehensible innovation, even if there is no proof indicating it being reprehensible by nature.*
>
> *They do so clinging to the Hadith 'Be weary of newly invented matters' while they seem unaware that what is meant by this is to make a matter which is contrary to the faith into something integral to it." [al-Taftazani, Sharh al-Maqasid, v2 pg 271].*

Living the Law 2

Case Studies: *Understanding the application of Islamic Law in the modern age*

Module Slw 2.05.D

Lesson 1
Organ donation

Lesson 1

Aim: By the end of this lesson, students will become acquainted with the discussion amongst scholars relating to the legality of organ donations and the various issues related to the permissibility of the use of the human body for the benefit of others.

Objectives.
By the end of this lesson, students should be able to display the ability to:
1. **Outline** the basic definitions related to what is meant by organ donation.
2. **Summarize** the main points used by those who that do not permit the practice of organ donations.
3. **Provide** an analysis of these points, according to the opinions of the those scholars that allow such procedures.
4. **Summarize** the main points used by those that permit the practice of organ donation.
5. **Mention** the conditions that must be met in order for organ donation to be allowed.
6. **Discuss** the difference between *cardiac death* and *brain stem death* and why this distinction is of importance when discussing the issue of organ transplantation.

---

1. The issue of organ donation

> *"Therefore We prescribed for the Children of Israel that whoso slays a soul not to retaliate for a soul slain, nor for corruption done in the land, it shall be as if he had slain mankind altogether; and whoso gives life to a soul, it shall be as if he has given life to mankind altogether" (Al-Ma'idah:32)*

> *"We have dignified the Children of Adam and transported them around on land and at sea. We have provided them with wholesome things and favored them over many of those We have created." (Al-Isra:70)*

One of the most widely researched areas of contemporary Islamic law is that of medicine, where modern advances have led to the appearance of a number of legal and ethical dilemmas that require to be addressed from the perspective of Islamic law. Amongst these is the issue of organ donation: either from a person who donates part of their body to save the life of another, or allow an individual to retain the use of a vital organ.

Classical Islamic law has a dearth of material which touches upon some of the issues of concern in medicine today. How do these sources provide an insight into the issue of organ transplants, and to what degree is the material directly relevant to the issue at hand?

1.1 Basic definitions

1.1.1 An 'organ' is defined as any part of a person - tissues, cells, blood and so on - whether it is still attached or has been separated.
1.1.2 The use or benefit that is under discussion here is a benefit dictated by *necessity* to keep the beneficiary alive or to keep some essential or basic function of his body working.

2. The evidence of those that forbid organ donation

There are a number of recurring points made by scholars that have outlawed such procedures. These can be summarised into the following points:

2.1 Human sanctity (*hurmah*) and respect

> *"And verily we have honoured the children of Adam" [al-Isra:70]*

2.1.1 Prohibition of harm

> *The Prophet of God ﷺ said: "Breaking the bone of a dead person is tantamount to breaking the bone of a living person." [Abu Dawud, 3205; Ibn Majah, 1616].*

44

Commenting on this, the hadith scholar al-Tibi said *'This tradition indicates that the sin associated with breaking a bone is the same whether the person is alive or dead, so a dead person should not be disrespected just as a living person should not.'* A similar explanation of the hadith is given by the Andalusian Ibn Abd al-Barr who commented *"One can deduce from this that after their death they experience pain just as they do during their lifetime. They also experience joy as in life."* [al-Dihlawi, Injah al-Hujjah fi Sharh Ibn Majah, v1, 642]

2.1.1.1 Context of the hadith

Imam al-Suyuti, in his gloss on *Sunan Abi Dawud,* mentioned the context of the hadith. Jabir [ibn Abdillah] related: *'We accompanied the Messenger of God with a janazah to the graveyard and sat at the side of a grave. Those that were digging brought out a shin bone or the like and started to break it down. The Messenger ﷺ said 'Do not do so! Breaking the bone of a dead person is tantamount to breaking the bone of a living person. Put it at the side of the grave."*

2.1.2 Prohibition on utilisation (manfa'ah) and sale of the human body

The sanctity of the human body has other ramifications as well. It is not permitted that the human body be made use of or sold.

> *"It is not permitted that the bones and hair of the human being be the object of a sale contract. This is not because they are impure, as they are pure according to the most correct view. Rather this is out of respect for them, since offering something for sale carries the meaning of humiliation (ihanah) and disrespect."* [Al-Kashani, Badai al-Sana'i, v5, p142].

2.1.3 Text analysis:

> ***"...As for what we are discussing concerning the permissibility of utilising parts of a body, then this is not considered to be disrespectful (ihana').*** *One cannot construe the hadith to mean this. Rather it may well be that it constitutes the honouring of the deceased through the preservation of one of his organs so that a living person may benefit from it. The living person is better than the deceased and they may have a reward recorded for this action. Even if, for argument's sake, one concedes that this constitutes disrespect, forbidden things may be permitted in cases of necessity. If two negative things are mutually exclusive then the least disruptive of these is allowed, based on an analogy of other similar issues such as [utilising] different types of prohibited medication or consuming carrion meat as well as other things [that are permitted] in states of compulsion..."* [Sh. Ibrahim al-Yaqubi, Shifa al-Tabarih, pp33-34].

2.2 Such operations are tantamount to mutilation (muthla)

> *"I will mislead them and I will order them to slit the ears of cattle, and to deface the (fair) nature created by God."* [An-Nisa:119]

> Samurah ibn Jundub narrates that *"The Messenger ﷺ used to encourage the giving of charity and forbade Muthla."* [Abu Dawud]

Some scholars also hold that saving the life of an unborn child in the womb is not permitted, based on it being akin to mutilation.

> *"The proof of our position is that this child does not usually survive. It is also not certain whether the child is alive in the first instance. Therefore it is not permitted that one breach a definite sanctity (hurmatan mutayaqinah) for one that is merely envisaged (mawhumah). The Prophet ﷺ said "Breaking the bone of a dead person is tantamount to breaking the bone of a living person." [Abu Dawud] and he ﷺ forbade mutilation (muthlah)."* [Ibn Qudamah, al-Mughni, V2, 413-4]

2.2.1 Text analysis:

The concept of mutilation is, in Islamic law, limited to the act of dismembering and disfiguring a dead body in war, out of spite or enmity. It is '*...a term reserved for heinous disfigurement such as smashing the head, cutting of the ears or nose."* [al-Dardir, Sharh al-Kabir, v2, p179]

It was expressly forbidden in cases such as war and armed conflict, as it runs contrary to upholding the sanctity of the human body in life and death.

Medical procedures involved in the extraction of a vital organ after one's death are not comparable to mutilation, as the underlying reason and physical procedure in which this is done are different. Also, the prohibition of saving a fetus in the womb is not universally accepted, and cannot be held to be mutilation, based on other legal texts quoted here.

> "It is stated in the legal edicts (fatawa) of Abu Layth [al-Samarqandi] regarding a pregnant woman who died - and it is known that the child within her womb is alive: 'One cuts open the stomach from the left side. This is also the case if it is most probable that the child is alive. This is similarly reported in al-Muhit[23]. It is related that this was done once with the expressed permission of Abu Hanifah, and the child lived.'" [Fatawah al-Hindiyah v5 pg 360. Quoted in Shifa al-Tabarih, p66]

2.3 Legal maxims[24]

> "When the evidences of prohibition conflict with the evidences of permissibility, preference is given to prohibition."

> "Harm cannot be removed by a similar harm."   [Ibn Nujaym, al-Ashbah wa al-Naza'ir]

Text analysis: "The truth is that in a state of compulsion, what is initially forbidden ceases to have the ruling of prohibition and is given the ruling of either permissibility or obligation. Therefore, it is only correct to draw an analogy based upon other cases so that the prohibition is lifted and the issue is conferred the ruling of either permissibility or obligation. An example of this is the Qur'anic verse in which God has forbidden carrion, blood and the flesh of swine [...] the ruling of prohibition has been lifted in a state of dire need [...].

Drawing an analogy for treating oneself through transferring some organs on the case of seeking treatment through what is forbidden or impure is a valid analogy, since seeking treatment through the prohibited or impure in a state of compulsion (darurah) removes the ruling of prohibition and the issue is given the ruling of permissibility or obligation. Similarly, treatment through organ transfer removes the ruling of prohibition [...].

This is how one should understand the words of God, may He be Exalted, and the words of legal scholars and jurist consultants." [Sh Ibrahim al-Yaqubi, Shifa al-Tabarih, p38].

2.4 Islamic legal philosophy: humans do not have ownership of their own bodies

This means that God has a right over the human body, as He created and fashioned humans and perfected their form. Humans are not given the permission to interfere in this right of God.

> "The preservation of one's life, perfecting one's intellect and body are from the rights that God has over mankind, and not from the rights of man per se [...]. It is God that nurtures perfection in a person through their life, body and intellect by which they attain what they are obliged to do. It is not allowed for the individual to forfeit this." [al-Shatibi, al-Muwafaqat, v2, 373].

3. The proofs of those who advocate the permissibility of organ donation

3.1 Public interest and altruism (*ithar*)

This is based both on the concept of *maslaha* and the common good. Also of relevance is the intention of receiving a reward by helping someone in need by forfeiting one's own personal rights (altruism). *Maslahah* literally means 'benefit or interest'. Al-Ghazzali defined it as the procurement of benefit and repulsing of harm. Islamic law seeks to preserve five essential elements of human life. These are, in descending order of priority: religion, life, intellect, lineage, property. [al-Mustasfa, 1[4]-258].

---

[23] The 25 volume work on Hanafi fiqh named *al-Muhit al-Burhani* by Burhan al-Din Muhammad ibn Mazah al-Bukhari, (d.616 AH)

[24] See Shari'ah module 1 lesson 6

The correct use of *maslahah* would require taking into account the five essentials of human life, together with a consideration of the public interest, before arriving at a ruling. *[al-Mustasfa, 2[4]-139].*[25]

3.2 Legal maxims

There are also a number of classical legal maxims that point to the permissibility of organ donation:

3.2.1 Prohibitions are waived in cases of necessity (*darurah*)

> *"He has only forbidden you dead meat, and blood, and the flesh of swine, and that on which any other name has been invoked besides that of God. But if one is forced by necessity, without willful disobedience, or transgressing due limits, then he deserves no rebuke. For God is Most Forgiving, Most Merciful." [2:173]*

> *"Necessity makes what is prohibited lawful." [al-Suyuti, al-Ashbah wa al-Naza'ir]*

There are a number of cases of necessity in which scholars have agreed that one may cut open a dead body. The original prohibition is waived and it is permitted based on a verifiable necessity.

> *"The Shafi'i scholars permit the exhuming of a grave for a number of reasons, such as if the grave contains wealth belonging to somebody else, or if the person had swallowed an item of wealth either of his own or somebody else's. In these cases it is permitted to split open the stomach. Similarly, if a woman was buried whilst having a foetus within her womb which could be saved, it would be obligatory to cut open her stomach, as has been mentioned by al-Nawawi." [Sh. Ibrahim al-Yaqubi, Shifa al-Tabarih, pp82-83].*

3.2.1.1 Consuming human flesh in a state of dire necessity

The other issue of relevance in the discussion of the sanctity of the human body is the consumption of a human corpse by one with no other means to avoid death.

There is no unanimity concerning the question at hand. Shafi'i scholars, Abu Khattab of the Hanbali school and Qadi Abu Bakr Ibn Al-Arabi and Ibn 'Arafah from amongst the Maliki scholars permitted a person in dire need to consume from the dead body of a human being if such an action would benefit them. The majority of jurists do not consider this as being permissible under any circumstances. The reasoning of both parties is based on the same reasoning mentioned above.

The reasoning of the majority is that the human being is to be honoured, whether alive or dead, and the Prophetic tradition which states *"The breaking of a dead person's bone is tantamount to breaking it while they are alive."* The proof of those that have permitted this is that the honour due to the living is greater than that due to the dead. They also add that the detrimental effects relating to consuming a dead corpse are less than those related to allowing a living person to die. *[See Yasin, Abhath al-Fiqhiyyah fi qadaya tibiyyah muasirah, p142]*

3.2.2 Lesser of two evils

> *"If two harmful and detrimental actions (mafasid) are mutually exclusive, then the least harmful and detrimental is given preference"*

The scope of Human sanctity after death is not universal in its scope, since scholars have discussed in detail the circumstances in which one may both exhume as well as split open a dead corpse. The legal maxim above indicates that there are situations in which scholars have agreed that one may cut open a dead body. Amongst those mentioned is to recover wealth that has been buried with the dead body or known to have been swallowed. They also mention the case of saving a fully formed fetus in the womb - as mentioned above.

> *"Opening up the stomach of a corpse is permitted [to retrieve an] item of wealth which has been swallowed during their lifetime, after which they passed away with it remaining within the stomach. This is regardless of whether it belonged to them or to somebody else, as long as it has a large value [such] that it is comparable to the nisab of zakat. Ibn Qasim said, regarding a person who swallowed a jewel belonging to either themselves or somebody else: 'The stomach is opened if it is a considerable amount. [However] another time he said it is not split open even if it is great." [Al-Ulaysh, Fath al-'Ali al-Malik, v1 p319].*

----

[25] See Shari'ah module 1 lesson 3

4. Appendices

4.1 Edicts of the International Islamic Fiqh Academies on organ donation

As covered in the previous module, there are two main Islamic fiqh academies. One of them is based in Makkah, and the other in Jeddah. The Makkan academy functions under the auspices of the Muslim World League. The Jeddah academy is an organ of the Organization of the Islamic Conference (OIC). Its officials are drawn from member states and from other countries.

Proceedings of the International Islamic Fiqh Academy [*Jeddah*]

[1] It is permissible to transplant an organ from one place in a person's body to another place in the same body, but attention must be paid to ensuring that the expected benefits outweigh any possible harm; that is subject to the condition that this is done to replace a lost organ or body part, or to restore its regular shape or function, or to correct a fault or remove a deformity that is causing the person psychological or physical harm.

[2] It is permissible to transplant an organ from the body of one person to another if it is an organ that renews itself automatically, such as blood and skin. But attention must be paid to the condition that the donor be fully qualified and fulfill the shar'i conditions.

[3] It is permissible to make use of organs that have been taken from the body of another person due to sickness, such as taking the cornea from the eye of a person whose eye has been removed due to sickness.

[4] It is prohibited to transplant an organ on which life depends, such as transplanting the heart from a living person to another person.

[5] It is prohibited to transplant an organ from a living person when its removal may cause an essential function to cease, even though his life does not depend on it, such as taking the corneas of both eyes. But if he will still have partial function [of the organ] after removing it, then the matter is subject to further discussion as we shall see below in section 8.

[6] It is permissible to transplant an organ from a dead person to a living person whose life or basic essential functions depend on that organ, subject to the condition that permission be given by the deceased before his death, or by his heirs after his death, or by the authorities in charge of the Muslims if the identity of the deceased is unknown, or he has no heirs.

[7] It should be noted that the agreement on the permissibility of organ transplants explained above is subject to the condition that this is not done by selling the organs, because it is not permissible to subject human organs to sale under any circumstances. For the beneficiary spending money in order to obtain the required organ where necessary, or offering compensation or honouring the donor, is subject to ijtihad and further discussion.

[8] All cases having to do with this topic are subject to further research and discussion, and they should be studied and discussed in a future session in the light of medical data and shar'i rulings. And God knows best. [Majma' al-Fiqh al-Islami, Qararat, P. 59-60; 18-23 Safar 1408 AH/6-11 February 1988 CE]

At its eighth working session, the Islamic fiqh Academy of the Muslim World League based in Makkah, also declared the permissibility of homotransplants[26] *(removing the organ from one person and transplanting it into another person's body)* to keep the beneficiary alive or to keep some essential or basic function of his body working.

4.2 The signs of death

When can we say that a person is dead? The traditional criterion followed by *Islamic legal scholars* has always been related to the heart; the stopping of circulation and respiration - known as *cardiac death*.

Modern medical advances point to brain stem death[27] as the ultimate criteria that determines the end of life and it is on this that medical science bases its judgment on death.

Both criteria are closely related: brain stem death takes place shortly after the cessation of circulation and respiration which, after the brain dies, can only be maintained artificially. This issue is of importance as the harvesting of organs from a brain stem dead body can only successfully take place if the life support system is on, leading to a scenario where the person is declared clinically dead according to one criteria (Medical) but not strictly speaking according to the other (Islamic).

---

[26] It also declared as permissible heterotransplants out of necessity - the transplantation of the organ of an animal into a human, if it has been slaughtered according to Islamic law.

[27] "Brain death" as a type of medically and legally acceptable death was first put forward with the 1968 Harvard report becoming the "standard" definition of brain death *[Report of the Committee of the Harvard Medical School to Examine the Definition of Brain Death. Jama, 1968; 205(6): 337–40]*

> *"...The law academies of the Organization of the Islamic Conference (IOC) (1986) and the Muslim World League (MWL) (1987) commented on the problems associated with legitimizing the brain death criterion in each case in the form of a qarar (decision). The underlying question about being allowed to turn off the respirator due to a diagnosis of brain death had, in the western context, already led to the recognition that the actual question pointed in the opposite direction: was it permissible to artificially prolong the respiration and circulation of a person who had been declared dead due to the brain-death criteria in order to guarantee a medically flawless organ harvest?" [Grundmann, Shari`ah, Brain Death, and Organ Transplantation, Orient, vol. 45, no. 1 (2004): 27]*

There has not yet been a clear and unanimous edict regarding the permissibility of retrieving organs from patients clinically diagnosed as being brain stem dead, whilst being artificially kept alive. Some scholars state that both types of death are necessary for a person to be declared dead in Islamic law. This means that organs cannot be taken from a person who is alive according to either definition. Those scholars who do not consider brain death to be the definitive sign of death naturally do not allow for organ harvesting from brain dead patients, as they consider them to have some vestige of life.

There are those who acknowledge brain death as a form of death and equate it to irreversible *cardio-respiratory* arrest (cardiac death). Shaykh Muhammed al-Salami, the former Mufti of Tunisia, wrote in favour of the permissibility of retrieving organs from patients clinically diagnosed as being brain stem dead based upon accepting brain stem death as the ultimate criteria signalling the end of human life [28]. In 1986, the third international conference of Islamic jurists held in Amman passed a resolution *[No.86-07-3D (5)]* which equated brain stem death with cardiac death, a resolution that paved the way for routine transplants from those kept alive artificially after having been pronounced brain stem dead.[29]

4.3 Wills and organ donation

4.3.1 Donation of a human organ through a will

> *"[T]he scope for permission is much larger than that [which] we reviewed for the donation of organs while alive. That is so because the worst harm in the donation of human organs is not present in that form of donation, namely the harm of damaging present life and exposing it to unnecessary risks and dangers. There is no life in the dead that we may threaten by the taking of their organs." [The Rulings for the Donation of Human Organs in the Light of Shari'a Rules and Medical Facts, Mohammad Naeem Yaseen, Arab Law Quarterly, Vol. 5, No. 1 (Feb., 1990), pp49-87]*

4.3.2 Seeking the permission of the relatives

Although not expressly stated, there is a general consensus in the literature that the relatives of the deceased have a say in allowing for an organ to be taken from the body, even if there is no will or donor instruction to that effect. Relatives also seem to be afforded the right to object to the harvesting of an organ, even if the deceased has left specific instructions consenting to such a procedure.

> *'Obtaining the permission of the relatives of the deceased allowing the operation to take place is not because they have control over the dead body, or because they inherit the corpse, but because tampering with the corpses may have an effect upon them by harming them emotionally. The legal maxim states that harm is to be removed. They also have the right to protect the sanctity of their dead, as has been stated before. Similarly, moving to remove organs from a dead person without the approval of their family and relatives may lead to disputes as well as entering into controversy with them, whereas God has ordered us to stay clear of disputes. Considering this, it is necessary that both the permission of the dead person as well as the agreement of the family be obtained. If the deceased has given permission and the relatives and family insist on not allowing it, then the organ may not be taken." [as-Saba'i, at-Tabib - Adabuhu wa Fiqhuhu, p223, Dar al-Qalam, 2005]*

---

[28] M. al-Salami, "Mata Tantahi al-Hayat," *Majallat Majma` al-Fiqh al-Islami*, no. 3, 687.

[29] The most up to date writings dealing with organ donation have revisited the standing of the brain stem death criteria, with the extensive fatwa of Mufti Mohammed Zubayr Butt ultimately viewing it as insufficient to pronounce a person dead for the purpose of organ donation. *[Butt, Mufti Mohammed Zubair, Organ Donation and Transplantation in Islam, 2019]*. The alternative position presented thoroughly by Shaykh Dr Rafaqat Rashid, falls in line with most international fatwa councils and the position set out in these class notes since being written in 2011, namely viewing brain stem criteria as a definitive and final indicator of death in the context of Islamic law. *[Rashid, R. Islamic Response to the Debate on Organ Transplant: Bodily Dignity, Neurological Death and the Dead Donor Rule, London: Al-Balagh Academy Publication Papers, 2020]*

Lesson 2
The issue of music - Part 1

Lesson 2

Aim: By the end of this lesson, students should become aquatinted with the discussion amongst scholars relating to the legality of music, in particular those that place restrictions on its usage.

Objectives.
By the end of this lesson, students should be able to display the ability to:
1. **Outline** the background to the discussion over the use of music in the context of the shari'ah.
2. **Mention** the Qur'anic verses used by those that place restrictions on its usage and discuss whether the verses are conclusive and definitive in the meanings they convey (*qati' al-dalalah*), or inconclusive and speculative (*dhanni al-dalalah*).
3. **Mention** the Prophetic hadith used as evidence by those that place restrictions on its usage
4. **Discuss** the *isnad* of the hadith *"There will be, from my community, people that will declare the legality of fornication, silk, wine and musical instruments (m'aazif)."*
5. **Discuss** the *matn* of the same hadith and whether the meaning conveyed is conclusive and definitive (*qati' al-dalalah*) or inconclusive and speculative (*dhanni al-dalalah*).
6. Summarize the standing of the hadith that point to the prohibition of music.

---

1. The background

The debate over the degree to which songs and music have a basis in both the religious and mundane life of the Muslim community has been well documented in classical sources. Games such as chess, songs, the use of musical instruments and even poetry in public gatherings have attracted scholarly debate based on the Qur'an's condemnation of pastimes that distract from the remembrance of God. Poetry, song and music are closely related, as poetry is the natural prerequisite of song. A song requires that which is sung and the rhythmic prose that form the basis of poetry are taken by some to be condemned in the light of the Qur'anic reproach of poets ***"and as for the poets that follow others into evil, do not see that they wander distracted in every valley and that they say what they practice not" [Ash-Shu'ara:224]***.

As always, in understanding a religious text, context is of paramount importance. Are the verses to be taken literally, or do scholars look at the underlying intent they convey? What is clear from the Prophetic *sunnah* is that these verses were targeted at those poets who preached falsehood and enmity, and not those who exhorted to good conduct and spoke for the truth. The case of Hasan bin Thabit or Abdullah ibn Rawaha is particularly important, as they were exhorted to write poetry both in defense and praise of the Prophet and Islam. What was condemned was the content and not the form itself.

The underlying reason why an action was carried out is of particular importance when looking at the contemporary discussion on the permissibility of various forms of *nashid* (devotional songs) in promoting the message of Islam. These two lessons aim only to provide a summary presentation of both sides of the discussion, focusing on the principal points. By presenting one of the main points in a degree of detail, this method will hopefully provide a faithful summary of the discussion from both sides.

2. Qur'anic proofs of those that prohibit the use of music and song

2.1. *'Futile distracting speech'*

> *"And from amongst mankind there are those who purchase futile distracting speech that they may mislead people from the way of God and make a mockery of it, for such people there is a humiliating punishment." [Luqman:6]*

The early authority on Qur'anic commentary, Imam al-Tabari, related that the words in the verse *"futile distracting speech"* refer to the songstresses: this opinion is generally related from many early commentators. The context in which the verses were revealed further clarifies the meaning. One narration related that one of the staunchest enemies of Islam, Nadr ibn Harith, commissioned people to sing and play music to divert people's attention from the preaching of the early Muslims. Another version has it that he would relate Persian fables to the people to distract them from the message of Islam. The actual word used in the verse *"lahw"* means 'anything through which a person is amused and distracted, forgetting more important and significant issues'. [Al-Alusi, Tafsir Ruh al-Ma'ani, v21, p67]

Al-Hasan Al-Basri was reported as saying that *"lahw al-hadith"* includes *"everything which distracts one from worship and the remembrance of God, such as wasting the night away in idle conversation or entertainment, jokes, superstitious tales, songs and the like thereof" [Al-Alusi, Ruh al-Ma'ani, v21, pp66-7]*

According to al-Tabari, this is either:

- A reference to the sale of instruments of amusement, hiring of songstresses and listening to such things. The following is related from the companion Ibn Masud *"By the one other than whom there is no God, it refers to singing! He repeated these words three times." [at-Tabari, Jami al-Ahkam, v 18, p535]*
- A reference to any conversation consisting of *shirk* (polytheism). This was the view of some tafsir scholars from the generation after the Companions, such as al-Dahhak and Abdur-Rahman bin Zayd. *[ibd. v 18, p538]*

> *"The most correct view regarding the meaning of 'lahw al-hadith' is that it indicates every form of conversation which diverts from God's path - the hearing of which has been prohibited by God or His Messenger ﷺ. This is because the statement by God, the exalted, is general and inclusive, and does not exclude certain forms of conversation. Therefore, His statement remains in its general context unless proof appears which specifies it. Singing and polytheism (shirk) are included in this general statement." [at-Tabari, Jami al-Ahkam, v 18, p534, Also see Ibn al-Arabi, Ahkam al-Quran, v3, p526]*

2.2 'The voice of Satan'

> **"...lead to perdition whomsoever you are able to by means of your voice"** *[Al-Isra:64].*

While the word in question here for 'voice' (*sawt*), literally means 'a sound or a voice', early commentators have explained this in various ways. *'Ibn Abbas took it to mean ' ...the voice of every person who calls others to disobedience to God.' Mujahid said 'What is meant by 'voice' is singing and [the] flute', while al-Hassan al-Basri stated that it was the drum, as related by Ibn Abi Hatim." [al-Suyuti, al-Iklil fi istinbat al-Tanzil', v2, p919]*

2.3 'Oblivious song'

> **"And do they wonder over this speech - laughing at it, and do not weep - treating life as a game (samidun)"** *[An-Najm:59-61]*

This verse refers to condemning people who are diverted from the Qur'an and mock it, preferring instead distractions and vanity. The word **samid** in Arabic can have various meanings, the most prominent of which is *'to stand up proudly or in a distractive manner' [al-Sihah]*. This is the most common use of the word. It is also mentioned that the word *samidun* is equivalent to *'khamidun'*, which means *'silent and motionless'*.

Those that seek to use this verse as a proof against music and singing mention that in certain classical Arabic dialects, *samid* conveys the meaning of singing (*ghina*). *[See Ibn Mandhur, Lisan al-Arab]*

2.4 The General conclusion of Qur'anic proofs

Although the verses used to argue against recitals are, by their nature, established texts, they are still conjectural and non-definitive (*dhanni al-dalalah*) in the meaning they convey. This is based upon the fact that there are numerous possible interpretations of the verses as shown above.

3. Prophetic traditions indicating prohibition of music and song

3.1 'Wine and musical instruments'

> Abu Musa said that he heard the Prophet ﷺ say 'There will be from my community people that will consider as lawful: fornication (al-hir), silk, wine and musical instruments (ma'azif)..." [Bukhari, 5590].

3.1.1 The sanad

The first narrator in the chain from al-Bukhari is Hisham ibn Ammar, who died in the year 245, and resided in ash-Sham.

He related from *Saddaqa ibn Khalid* on the authority of *Abdul Rahman ibn Yazid* from *Attiyah ibn Qays*, whose source for the hadith was Abdul Rahman ibn Ghanam al-Ashari, who died in the year 78 and who initially resided in Medina, but was sent by the second Caliph to Damascus in order to educate people there. He related the hadith from one of two Companions (or both): *Abu Malik or Abu Amir al-Ashari* on the authority of the Prophet ﷺ. *[See Ibn Hajar, Tahdib al-Tahdhib]*

3.1.1.1 Criticisms of the sanad by Ibn Hazm

Ibn Hazm sought to criticise the hadith on two accounts *[al-Muhala, v9, p332]*:

Firstly al-Bukhari, when relating from his first authority, said that "Hisham said". Ibn Hazm considered al-Bukhari to have not heard the hadith directly from Hisham ibn 'Ammar, since the words of al-Bukhari were *"Hisham ibn 'Ammar said"* and not *'I heard him say"*. In other words, he did not express that he heard him say this.

This is technically considered a break in the chain. It should be remembered that in hadith science, the issue of the words used when relating from another authority are of importance when a source is known to be *disingenuous (mudalis)* with regards to their own sources. If al-Bukhari wanted to hide the fact that he had not heard this from Hisham, he would use words such as *'Hisham said'* instead of *'I heard him say'* hoping that no one would pick up on this slight difference. Such *disingenuousness* can lead to the hadith being declared as being broken and so weak. This is because there may have been a person between the two narrators left unnamed, with the chances being that this unknown person was weak.

The question arises: did al-Bukhari meet Hisham, and was al-Bukhari known to be *disingenuous (mudalis)*? The hadith specialist Ibn Salah said:

> *"These criticisms from Ibn Hazm are unfounded for a number of reasons:*
>
> *1- This hadith has no break in the chain, since al-Bukhari had met Hisham as well as hearing [hadith] from him. We have made clear in our book 'The sciences of Hadith' that if one verified that two people have both met and heard from each other and are not accused of being disingenuous (mudalis), then one should take what is related as being an example of direct hearing (sama') regardless of the words used in the hadith. This is similar to taking the hadith to be an example of direct hearing (sama') when a Companion says 'The Prophet of God **said'** if there is no indication to the contrary.*
>
> *2- This hadith is well known to be unbroken (muttasil) because of numerous other chains of narration that clearly indicate that they met.[30]*
>
> *3- Even if we do term it as having a type of break, these types of narration that appear in the two collections [of Imam al-Bukhari and Muslim] are not defined as having a break which impairs [authenticity] (inqita' qadih). This is on account of what we know of the methodology and conditions employed by them both, which leads them to include only such narrations in their books which are stringently authenticated." [al-Nawawi, Sharh Muslim, v1, p134]*

The second criticism Ibn Hazm made of the hadith was regarding the Prophetic Companion (*sahabi*) from whom Abdul Rahman Ibn Ghunum related the hadith. He said *'either Abu Amir or Abu Malik al-Ashari narrated to me - and by God he did not lie to me- that he heard the Prophet ﷺ say…"*

From this version of the hadith, there seems to be a degree of doubt as to which Companions the hadith is related from. This criticism is seen by the majority of scholars as being irrelevant, since any doubt over the identity of the Companion would not affect the authenticity of the hadith itself. This is because all Companions are considered upright and trustworthy[31].

> *"This is an authentic hadith. It has no deficiency or defect, and there is no point of weakness upon which any attack be made. Abu Muhammad Ibn Hazm labeled it defective by virtue of his claim that there is a break (intiqaa) in the chain between Al-Bukhari and Sadaqah bin Khalid; and because of the difference of opinion regarding the name of Abu Malik [...]. As*

---

[30] *"If al-Bukhari had not heard this from him, he would not have held it permissible to use such a definitive phrase. al-Bukhari did relate directly from Hisham and received hadith from him," [Ibn Qayyim, Ighatha al-Lahfan v1, p220]*

[31] See Hadith module lesson two.

for the difference regarding the kunyah[32] of the Companions [Abu Amir or Abu Malik], they are all of impeccable stature. Furthermore, in the narration of Ibn Hibban, the transmitter stated that he heard from both of them." [Ibn Hajr, Taghliq at-Ta'liq, v5, pg 17; Fath al-Bari, v10 p68]

3.1.2 The matn

3.1.2.1 The inconclusive meaning of 'ma'azif'

"By 'azf' [what] is meant [is] playing with mazif, consisting of the duff (hand drum) or other instruments which are struck (i.e percussion instruments). It may also be used more generically to mean any idle amusement (la'ib)." [Ibn al-Athir, An-Nihayah, 2:200]

In the dictionary Lisan al-Arab, *maa'zif* are stated to be musical instruments which are struck. If the singular form is used (*mi'zaf*), it specifically means a long stringed instrument used mainly by the people of Yemen. The flute is sometimes referred to as a *mi'zaf*. [v3, p2609; al-Shaukani, Nayl al-Awtar, v8, p106]

3.1.2.2 Wording of the hadith on 'wine and musical instruments'

The discussion revolves around a few key points:

- The variations in the wording of this hadith amongst different authorities. Abu Dawud related this hadith [§4039] with the same chain from Ibn Yazid, but did not mention the last three words including *maa'zif*, and had the word *al-khiz (brocade)* instead of *al-hir (fornication)*[33]. There are also differences in some of the other words used. Does this make the hadith weak on account of the inconsistency (*idtirab*) in wording? The general rule in hadith science, is that if a hadith has variants that include extra details, they are accepted if they are related by competent narrators (*ziyad al-thiqat maqbul*). [See al-Shaukani, Nayl al-Awtar, v8, p107]

- The phrase in the hadith *'consider as lawful' (yastahillun)'*, according to Qadi Abu Bakr Ibn Al-Arabi, could have one of two distinct meanings:

  First: Such people will hold these to be lawful *(the literal meaning)*.
  Second: It could be that a metaphorical meaning be given for the phrase *'consider as lawful'*. The metaphorical meaning being that of *'exceeding the limits (istirsal).'*

  The implication of his words is that the metaphorical meaning is given precedence, because if the literal meaning was intended, people that permitted musical instruments would have to be deemed disbelievers (for holding halal something that is clearly haram). However no one has said that those who permit musical instruments are outside the fold of Islam. *[al-Shaukani, Nayl al-Awtar, v8, p106; also see Ibn Hajar, Fath, v10, p70]* [34]

3.2. 'The shepherd's flute'

Nafi' related that Abdullah ibn Umar heard the sound of a shepherd's flute and so put his fingers in his ears and moved the camel he was riding away from the road, then he asked Nafi *"...Do you still hear it."* He said *'Yes'* and so Ibn Umar continued to ask until I said *'No'*. He then put his hand down and returned to the road saying *"I saw the Messenger ﷺ hear the sound of a shepherd's flute and he did this."* [Abu Dawud, 4924]

---

[32] Kunyah is a word used to describe a person by one of their children such as *Abu* 'father of' or *Umm* 'mother of'.

[33] The difference between the words is an extra dot on two of the letters

[34] Another point that is mentioned with relation to the matn of the hadith relates to the connection of items through the conjunctive article *'waw'* (and). Does this mean that they share a collective ruling of prohibition, or do they each have a separate ruling? *[al-Shaukani, Nayl al-Awtar, v8, p107]*. Scholars of juristic methodology do state that the mere fact that things are mentioned in the same context does not necessarily mean that they share the same ruling. Al-Kuwrani says in his didactic poem on legal methodology (*Nadhm Mukhtasar al-Manar*):

> *"and being coupled together in the context of a linguistic construction*
> *does not necessitate being coupled together in terms of the ruling"*

However, the reality is that all scholars of jurisprudence (usul) agree that singular words (mufradat) connected through conjunctive articles such as *'waw'* lead to all the words sharing the same ruling, as opposed to when sentences (jumal) are so connected. *[See al-Jasas, al-Fusul, v3, 263; Ibn Qudamah, Rawd al-Nadhir, v 1, p261; al-Baji, Ihkam, p373]*

3.2.1 Sanad

This hadith was stated by Abu Dawud as being *munkar (lit. frowned upon)* which usually means that it is weak. However, he gave no reason for such a ruling. *"This is what Abu Dawud states, but it is not known on what basis it is munkar, as all of the narrators are trustworthy (thiqat) and they are not contradicting stronger narrators." [al-Adhimabadi, Awn al-Ma'bud, v13, p267].* Abu Dawud may have meant that he could not find the narrators being corroborated in their narration by other *(la mutaba'a lahu)." [Ibn Qudamah, Mughni, v14, p159; al-Laknawi, Dhafar al-Amani, p362-4]*

3.3 "The drum"

Ibn Abbas reported the Prophet ﷺ to have said "Indeed God has prohibited wine, gambling and the kubah, and every intoxicant is haram". Sufyan, who was one of the narrators, said 'I asked my teacher (also one of the narrators) Ali ibn Badhimah what kubah is and he said 'the drum'" [Abu Dawud, 3696; also Ahmed, 2625].

Matn: The word *kubah* has been explained by one of the narrators of the hadith to mean the *tabl* (drum), and this is the meaning given to it by al-Jawhari in his dictionary *'al-Sihah'*. However this is not the only meaning of the word, as it is also said to mean backgammon *(nadr)*. *"Kubah is backgammon, while some say it is the drum or lute." [Ibn Athir, al-Nihayah, v2, p567]*

4. Review of proofs

There are many more hadith on this topic, such as what was related by Abu Hurayrah that the Prophet ﷺ said *"Angels do not accompany a caravan that has dogs or bells." [Muslim, 5546]* and *"The bell is the flute (mizmar) of the Satan." [Muslim, 5548].* A number of scholars have authored works on this. Those mentioned above are the most important Prophetic traditions indicating the prohibition of music. *[See also al-Shaukani, Nayl al-Awtar, v8, pp105-7]*

Scholars agree that the origin of all things is permissibility unless they are associated with acts of worship or marital affairs, in which case the default ruling is that of impermissibility.

However, as detailed above with pastimes such as singing and playing musical instruments, there are a number of religious texts which are used to restrict the permissibility of these acts.

Given this last point, what are the proofs that indicate this original permissibility? Are they conclusive and definitive in the meanings they convey (*qati' al-dalalah*) or are they inconclusive and speculative (*dhanni al-dalalah*).

Also, if they are Prophetic traditions, what is the level of authenticity of such hadith? Are they definitive or merely conjectural (*qati' al-thabut or dhanni al-thabut*) in terms of their authenticity? This will be looked at in the next lesson.

Lesson 3
The issue of music - Part 2

Lesson 3

Aim: By the end of this lesson, students will have become acquainted with the discussion amongst scholars relating to the legality of music and in particular, those that allow its usage.

Objectives.
By the end of this lesson, students should be able to display the ability to:
1. **Outline** the general proofs of those that allow the use of music and instruments.
2. **Mention** what is meant by *sama'* and what scholars say regarding its permissibility.
3. **Discuss** how these scholars respond to the hadith that condemn musical instruments.
4. **List** the main hadith proofs of those that allow the use of instruments.
5. **Discuss** the relevance of the hadith *'The children of Arfid'* in the debate on music.
6. **Mention** the *fiqh* opinions on what instruments are accepted and which are not.
7. **Explore** why the discussion on music is an issue within contemporary Islamic law.

Having looked at the main source texts for the restriction of song and music, this lesson will survey the text from the Qur'an and Prophetic sunnah that point to the permissibility of certain types of song and instruments.

1. Prophetic traditions indicating permissibility

It should be mentioned from the outset that there are no direct Qur'anic proofs put forward by those that hold music to be lawful. The main sources quoted are Prophetic traditions, the most important of which are mentioned below. None of these texts have been criticized because of their sanad, so there is little debate over the authenticity of the hadith mentioned. The main discussion relates to the meaning of the hadith and whether they indicate the permissibility of all instruments or just those mentioned in the narrations. Are the hadith restricted to particular events of happiness or are they applicable to all occasions, even if they are not specifically mentioned in hadith sources?

1.1 The hadith of 'Banu Arfidah'

> Aisha said: *"The Messenger ﷺ came to me when two girls were singing songs on Bu'ath. He then lay down on the bed and turned his face away, whereupon Abu Bakr entered and rebuked me saying "The musical instruments (mizmarah) of the Shaytan in the house of the Messenger of God!" The Messenger ﷺ turned to him and said "Leave them." A little later, when Abu Bakr was not paying attention, I signaled to them and they left."* [Al-Bukhari, 949]

> She said *"It was the day of Eid, the Abyssinians were playing in the mosque with shields and lances. Then either I asked the Messenger or he asked me whether I wanted to see them and I said yes. So he let me stand behind him with my cheek against his and he said "Continue on Banu Arfidah". When I was tired he asked "Is that sufficient for you?" I said "Yes". He then said "Then you can leave.""* [Al-Bukhari, 950].

The hadith of Aisha refers to two incidents that took place on the day of 'Eid, where two girls were singing in the room of Aisha about the battle of Bu'ath which took place between the Medinan tribes of Aws and Khazraj, around three years before the *Hijra*. Al-Zuhri also mentioned, in his version of the hadith, that they were also playing the duff, as supported by the narration of Imam Muslim. It also mentions that a group of Abyssinians were playing in a peculiar way to mark the day of 'Eid.

Here the Prophet ﷺ allowed expressions of celebration and merriment from a particular group of people in accordance with their cultural norms. As the Prophet ﷺ said: *"They are from the children of Arfid."*

> *"It is as though he meant that this was their particular style and as it was permissible, they should be left alone."* In other narrations of the hadith, it is related that the Prophet ﷺ said *"This is so in order that the Jews come to know that there is latitude within our religion."* [Ibn Hajar, Fath al-Bari v2, p573].

"The Prophet ﷺ covered his face, showing that he avoided partaking in this due to his elevated station, which required him not to pay attention to it. However, the fact that he did not censure this shows his granting general permissibility for this type of singing in the manner it was performed, because he would not have affirmed something that was wrong [...].

The general ruling on entertainment and distractive pastimes is that one should stay clear of them. As this instance runs contrary to this ruling, the exception to this rule is restricted to the time, qualities and degree of the exception shown in this instance and God knows best." [Ibn Hajar, Fath al-Bari v2, p571].

1.2 Returning from battle

Abdullah Ibn Buraydah said that he heard Buraydah say *'The Prophet ﷺ left for a battle and when he returned, a black female servant came to him and said "O Messenger of God! I had taken an oath that if God brought you back in safety that I would play the duff in your presence and sing." The Prophet ﷺ said to her "If you have indeed taken an oath then play, otherwise do not." She started to play the duff. Abu Bakr came in whilst she was doing so. Then 'Ali came in whilst she was beating the daff, then 'Uthman. Finally 'Umar came in and she threw the duff beneath herself and sat on it. The Messenger of God ﷺ said "The Shaytan is afraid of you, O 'Umar." [At-Tirmidhi, 3690, Ahmed]*

Al-Turbushti said, as is stated in the book 'The Sustenance for one seeking provisions regarding the commentary of at-Tirmidhi': "The only reason the Prophet ✉ allowed her to play in front of him was because she had taken an oath. The fact is that she took the oath - that if he ﷺ returned back in safety after having left - as being a blessing from God for her. Therefore, the ruling regarding this [i.e. playing] changed from it being a vain pastime to now having the quality of truth, and from being reprehensible to being something that was recommended." [al-Kattani, al-Taratib al-Idariyyah, v 2 p131].

1.3 The wedding of Rubiyah

This hadith is related by Rubiyah bint Mu'awwidh in which she said *"The Messenger ﷺ visited me the day I was to get married and sat on the bed even as you are sitting now. Some of our young girls were playing the duff and signing laments for my forefathers killed in Badr and one of them said 'Amongst us is a Prophet who knows what will happen tomorrow.' He ﷺ said "Leave that and continue in saying what you were saying before." [Bukhari, 5202].*

1.4 The hadith of the two Companions

Amir Sa'd said *"I came upon Qurazah ibn Ka'b and Abu Masud al-Ansari at a wedding, whereupon I found some young girls singing. I said to them "But you are from the Companions of the Prophet ﷺ and of those that were present at Badr, and this is done in your presence?" They said to him "Sit and listen with us if you wish or leave if you wish, we have been given permission for amusement in a wedding." [al-Nisai, 3385].*

1.5 The women of the Ansar

Aishah said *that she was present at the wedding ceremony of a woman from the Ansar, whereupon the Prophet ﷺ said to her "O Aisha, do you not have any form of amusement, for the Ansar are well disposed to amusements." [Bukhari, 5126].*

2. The general arguments of those that permit musical instruments

"If it is free from all prohibited things and safe from all suspicions and is not made a habit most of the time [...] it is permitted." [an-Nablusi, p62].

"It is haram to use or listen to musical instruments which those habituated to drink are known for, like the lute, cymbals, and the flute. The duff is permitted at weddings, circumcisions and other events even if it has bells on its sides, but the 'kubah' drum is unlawful." [al-Shurbini, Mughni al-Muhtaj, 4/429]

While some of those who allow the use of music may accept the religious texts mentioned regarding the condemnation of singing and instruments, they make the point that the context within which such statements were made was one where music and singing were inextricably linked with things that are without doubt haram. In this regard one can assume the following:

2.1 Music as a divergence. Music was used by those that had antagonism towards Islam as a tool to divert people from paying heed to the message, therefore it was prohibited by association and not intrinsically so.

2.2 Illicit associations. The general culture prevalent at the time made a clear connection between certain instruments, singing and the consumption of wine as well as congregating together in gatherings of ill-repute. This meant that due to the link and association that existed between what was clearly prohibited and condemned (i.e. wine, fornication...) and music, the early Muslims considered the condemnation of music as part and parcel of a condemnation of a culture of licentiousness and excess.

2.3 Slippery slope. There were clear misgivings regarding all types of recreational activity if they had no observable benefit, particularly when practiced to an extreme. For example, any activity that led to one delaying or missing the prayer was considered to deprive an individual of their ability to give legal evidence in court (*adalah*). A case in point is the issue of chess, which was taken by some scholars to be prohibited while others, attempting to understand the context within which it was condemned, made it a condition for its lawful use that one was punctual in the performance of the prayer and was not unduly preoccupied with chess.

Conclusion: Provocative lyrics, a culture of moral decadence and ill repute, the undue wasting of one's time, diverting oneself from one's obligations, both religious and moral, would all make any type of music or singing prohibited regardless of the type of instruments used, indeed regardless of the existence of instruments.

3. Imam al-Ghazali on the debate on music

Perhaps the most oft-quoted proponent in the debate on the permissibility of music is Imam al-Ghazali. He devoted a large section in his book *al-Ihya* to the permissibility of what is referred to as *sama'*. *Sama'* is the singing of spiritual songs and poems in a gathering for the benefit of those present. His arguments were as follows:

a. Commenting on the verse *"God will not take you to task for that which is unintentional in your oath" [Al-Baqarah:225]*, he stated that the word '*laghw*' indicates something that is harmless and therefore, music is one type of activity which is essentially harmless so it entails no sin.

b. *Sama'* is nothing other than the coming together of people in order to listen to words and rhythms that move the human heart. If none of the acts are prohibited in themselves, then how can a combination of these be condemned? As for the rhythm from which such *sama'* is constituted, he drew the analogy of the sounds that exist in nature that also have a pleasant rhythm such as the chirping of birds, with which mankind finds pleasure. They are permitted to listen to so why not this?

Some of the *Salaf* listened to singing of a type known as '*rajz*' - a rhythmic chanting which is not accompanied by musical instruments. Abdul Razaq al-Sanani' in his *Musanaf* reported: on the authority of Yahya ibn Sa'id that Sa'id ibn Musayyab said *"I hate ghina but love rajz."* [v 11, p4]. However, many early Muslims condemned both singing as well as the associated instruments. Abdullah ibn Masud said *'Ghina sows hypocrisy in the heart even as water grows vegetation."* Imam al-Ghazali commented on this statement of Ibn Masud saying that it actual refers to the one who sings in order to be praised by the audience. *[Ihya, v4, p496]*

4. Music and sama'

A large degree of the discussion regarding music is centred on the issue of devotional music (*sama'*) where religious poetry is sung or chanted either accompanied or unaccompanied by musical instruments. Of those that wrote favorably on this is the Hanafi lawyer 'Abdal Ghani an-Nablusi. He said:

4.1 'Abdal Ghani an-Nablusi on sama'.

> *"We say that sama' falls into three categories;*
> *first that which is haram, and relates to the majority of people - youth and all those whose desires and pursuit of pleasure have taken hold of them, the love of this world controls them, and whose inner selves have been muddied and their goals have been corrupted. Sama' does not excite within them [anything] except the base qualities that are dominant in their hearts. Especially in our times, with the corruption of our states and our deeds.*
> *The second category is mubah (permitted). It is for the one whose only share in it is the pleasure of listening to a good voice (i.e. with none of the ill effects), who seeks joy and reduction of his grief on the absence or death of someone.*

*The **third** category is mandub (recommended). It is for the person who has been overwhelmed by the love of God. Sama' excites only the noblest attributes in him and increases his desire for God. This is the sama' of the Sufis, the people of truth and sincerity."* [Al-Nabulsi, Idah al-Dalalat, p72].

5. The legal schools on the prohibition of music

Mohammed ibn Hatib reported that the Prophet ﷺ said *"The duff and singing in weddings distinguishes what is allowed from what is not." [Nisai, 3382].*

Abdul Hayy Al-Kattani said *"A number of scholars have authored books regarding sama' and singing - amongst them, Ibn Qutaybah, Abu Mansur at-Tamimi, Ibn Hazm...".* He mentioned over twenty scholars who have written at various lengths regarding the relative permissibility of certain types of singing and instruments. However, there is a wide degree of disagreement amongst them because of the general, legal positions of the schools of law have been critical of singing and instruments. *[Al-Kattani v 2 pp 132-135].*

The proofs given in lesson two were taken by the four schools of Sunni law as the basis of showing the prohibition of instruments, other than those that are expressly permitted. They argue that based on such texts, the ruling on instruments is that of prohibition unless a specific religious text exists showing an exemption. The rulings taken by the majority of classical scholars on both singing and musical instruments can be seen in the following summary.

5.1 Legal texts on singing and musical instruments

*"Musical instrumentation is of three types: that which **is forbidden (haram)** such as playing stringed instruments (awtar), extended flute (nay) as well as all wind instruments[35] (mazamir), the lute ('udd), mandolin (tunbur), the lyre (al-ma'zafah), rebec (rabab) and those that resemble these. Anyone who is habituated to listening to these thereby forfeits the right to have their testimony accepted. This is because it is related by Ali that the Messenger ﷺ said "If fifteen traits appear in my community then they will be afflicted with hardship..."[36] and mentioned the prominence of musical instrumentation [...].*

*There are those types which **are permitted (mubah)**. This specifically refers to the drum (duff) as the Messenger ﷺ said "Make public announcement of weddings and play the duff on such occasions" as related by Imam Muslim. The scholars of this (Hanbali) as well as the Shafi'i school have mentioned that it is reprehensible except at weddings [...].*

*[Lastly] for men to be playing the duff **is disliked (makruh)** since it was only women or effeminate males that used to play the duff. Such behavior would lead to men imitating women and the Prophet ﷺ cursed men that imitate women." [Ibn Qudamah, Mughni, v14, p157-9]*

6. General conclusions

6.1 The classical discussion can be aptly summed up by the words of the Yemeni jurist al-Shawkani:

"If one considers the arguments that we have put forward from both parties, it is obvious that even if the actual point that is being debated (mahal al-niza'a) is cleared from being declared within the ambit of the haram, it is still not cleared of doubt. Believers hold back when faced with doubtful matters, as made clear by the authentic hadith: 'Whoever has stayed clear of it has protected his honor and his religion. And whoever wanders around a preserve is likely to fall into it'[...]. So what [would be the ruling] if it contains mention of physical traits, of cheeks, beauty, flirting, of shunning a person then getting back together, sexual virility and impotency, of deflowering virgins? A person who listens to the like of this is hit with an enormous affliction (baliyyah) as it represents a degree of wanton callousness

---

[35] There are certain types of wind instruments that are differed upon, such as the *yara'* or shepherds' flute which, unlike the Iraqi flute, is usually played on its own, unaccompanied by stringed instruments. The Hanafi school state it to be *haram*, while the Maliki school mentions that in wedding festivities it, like the horn (*buq*) and flute (*zamara*), is disliked. The Shafi'i school have two variant positions on the *yara'*. Al-Rafi'i states: *Al-Baghawi has certified the position that it is haram, while al-Ghazali held it to be permitted, which seems to be the closer position as it provides added vigour when traveling. Al-Nawawi states that it is haram like all other instruments, as it is fully rhythmical on its own (mutrib bi-infiradihi).* [See Fatawa Hindiyyah, v5, p352; al-Dardir, sharh al-Saghir, v2, p325; Nihayah al-Muhtaj, v8, p281]

[36] al-Tirmidhi, 2210

towards God in a way that can barely be put into words." [al-Shaukani, Nayl al-Awtar, v8, p109]

6.2 The contemporary discussion on this issue relates to the changing nature of the relationship between music and culture and the ways in which music is utilized to spread and promote ideas. If we leave aside those types of music that are considered by all scholars to be haram on account of their lyrical content and negative associations, can other types of music be used to promote positive ideas through, say, Islamic nasheed?

What about background sounds for a documentary or film or an introductory theme tune to an educational T.V program? Does it make any difference if the sounds and music are computer generated?

The universal power of a mass media that strategically uses music for its own ends has led to contemporary scholars looking again at the question of whether music was initially prohibited for being inherently harmful, or whether it was due to the close association it had with other prohibited things such as lewdness, alcohol consumption and the like. On this question at least, scholars have clearly stated that musical instruments were forbidden due to their associated negative consequences, and not due to any inherent harm they have in themselves. *[See Ibn Abidin, Hashiyyah, v5, p223]*

As for those contemporary scholars who have permitted the use of musical instruments in today's environment, have they considered whether music can be separated from the negative aspects that have always been part of the music in the East; or from the negative aspects of general mass marketing in the West?

Lesson 4
The issue of meat

Lesson Four

Aim:
By the end of this lesson, the students should be able to understand the issues related to halal meat production and the questions that modern slaughtering techniques raise for Islamic law.

Objectives:
By the end of this lesson, the students should be able to display the ability to:
1.   Outline the main factors that have lead to the development of new animal slaughter methods.
2.   Discuss the rulings related to the one slaughtering according to Islamic law, and whether meat slaughtered by a Jew or a Christian is permitted for consumption by Muslims.
3.   State the difference of opinion regarding whether pronouncing the *tasmiyyah* by a Muslim is a condition for meat to be halal.
4.   State the difference of opinion regarding whether meat slaughtered by People of the Book must have the *tasmiyyah* pronounced on it by them for it to be halal.
5.   Explain why pronouncing the *tasmiyyah* over each animal when slaughtering it is necessary for meat to be halal, and whether modern slaughter techniques compromise this.
6.   Identify which arteries need to be severed for meat to be halal, and whether modern slaughter techniques compromise this.
7.   Explain what stunning entails and the ruling concerning this as discussed by scholarly bodies.

---

1. Introduction:

The issue of the Islamic legality of meat is not something that is a particularly modern concern. The Qur'an, as well as the Prophetic Sunnah, lays down guidelines on what is considered wholesome and what is not. The conditions that need to be fulfilled for meat to be halal have been examined in detail by classical scholars, but these conditions are also of relevance when looking at issues related to the permissibility of meat today. New techniques of slaughter have appeared based on changing demands for meat consumption and so these issues need to be revisited. These focus on two main factors:

   1.1 Animal welfare issues[37]. This has led the introduction of various types of pre-slaughter electric stunning. It is held that this alleviates animal suffering. In Islamic law, this raises the issue of the permissibility of such a technique before slaughter on the grounds of animal welfare.

   1.2 Market forces. The huge demand for meat products has meant the introduction of conveyer-belt technology in all areas of the slaughter process. In Islamic law, this type of mass production of meat raises key issues. What constitutes an acceptable slaughtering technique? Given that certain veins are required to be severed in the process of slaughter in religious law, can such a mechanical method be guaranteed to meet such criteria?

2. The Muslim law of halal meat [al-*dhabiha*]

The fiqh on which type of meat is considered halal and lawful is precise and can be detailed, but for the case study issue at hand, we can summarize the main concerns to revolve around three points of enquiry:

> *1. The one slaughtering.*
> *2. The severing of vital arteries.*
> *3. The animal being deemed alive at the time of slaughter*.

3. The one slaughtering

There are three issues of relevance here.
1- The religion of the one slaughtering.
2- The pronouncement of the *tasmiyyah (pronouncing bismillah)*
3 -*Tasmiyyah and machine slaughter*

---

[37] *Wider animal welfare issues related to rearing methods and the ethics of intensive farming are not part of the remit of this lesson. Dealing with the related ethical issues is, in many ways, more important than those discussed here.*

3.1 The religion of the one slaughtering.

An essential condition for meat to be considered halal is that the one slaughtering the animal be a Muslim or from the 'People of the Book' *(Ahl al-Kitab)*. The animal slaughtered by someone who is neither Muslim nor of the People of the Book is haram according to all the jurists. This is based on the following evidence:

> *"Today (all) things good and pure are made lawful for you. The food of the People of the Book is lawful for you and yours is lawful for them." (Al-Ma'idah:5)*

3.2 The pronouncement of the *tasmiyyah (pronouncing bismillah)*

3.2.1 Tasmiyyah of a Muslim

The majority of scholars hold that *tasmiyyah* is a condition for the correct slaughter of an animal by a Muslim based upon, amongst others, the following evidences:

> *"Do not consume that over which God's name has not been pronounced. For that would be sacrilegious." [Al-Anam:121]*

> *Rafi' ibn Khadij reported that the Messenger of God ﷺ said: 'If the instrument of slaughter causes the blood to gush out, and the name of God is pronounced, then eat it." [al-Bukhari, 5498]*

The Shafi'i school, however, does not stipulate that it is an essential condition that a Muslim mention *tasmiyyah* when slaughtering.

> *"It is recommended that the name of God be mentioned at the time of slaughter, as well as when one sends out hunting dogs or [fires] an arrow at prey. If one leaves out the tasmiyyah - either intentionally or by mistake, the animal and prey is halal. However, in the case of intentionally omitting tasmiyyah there are three different legal possibilities [awjuh]. [1] The most correct is that it is reprehensible [2] that it is not [3] it is a wrong action to do so." [an-Nawawi, al-Majmu', 9/61]*

They provide a number of proofs for the non-obligatory nature of the *tasmiyyah* - amongst them, the *Mursal* tradition in which al-Sal<u>t</u> [*a tabi'i*] related that the Messenger ﷺ said *'The animal slaughtered by a Muslim is halal, whether he mentions God's name or not, for if he was to do so he would not mention the name of anyone but God." [Abu Dawud, Marasil § 341]*

3.2.2 Tasmiyyah of the People of the Book

3.2.2.1 Who are the People of the Book?

The Shafi'i school has placed certain stipulations on what is meant by a Christian or Jew whose meat we may eat. They state that for a person to be considered as *Ahl al-Kitab* in this context they have to be from *'an ancient community that has not converted to the faith after the coming of a new Prophet'*. This means that communities that entered into Judaism after the coming of the Prophet Jesus (AS) or Christians that embraced Christianity after the coming of the Prophet ﷺ are not considered to belong to the *Ahl al-Kitab* as far as dietary laws are concerned. *[See Nihayat al-Muhtaj, v8,82-3]*

The majority of other scholars take the claim of anyone who professes to be from the Christian or Jewish faith on face value. As long as their co-religionists acknowledge them as such then they are 'People of the Book'. Ibn Taymiyyah said *"That an individual is from the People of the Book or not is understood from them and not their lineage. Anyone who professes the faith of the People of the Book is from them, even if it was their father or grandfather that initially converted. This is also the case if they converted after it was abrogated, altered or before this. This is the clear and stated position of [Imam] Ahmed." [al-Muqni', v3, p535]*.

If one is sure that the animal has not been slaughtered in the name of another deity or in the name of Jesus, it will be halal - provided the animal has been ritually slaughtered (as opposed to being beaten to death etc). *[See al-Kashani'i, Bada'i al-Sanai'i, v5, 46]*

3.2.2.1 Do the People of the Book have to mention the name of God when slaughtering?

It is disputed whether the meat of the Ahl al-Kitab is allowable for consumption if they do not pronounce the name of God over the animal at the time of slaughter.

a. **The Hanbali and Hanafi jurists** take the opinion that pronouncing the name of God is a condition for meat to be considered halal. They consider the verse allowing the consumption of the meat slaughtered by the People of the Book to be restricted by the verse which requires the mention of God's name over the animal at the time of slaughter.

> "The intentional mention of the name of God is a condition for every slaughtered animal, regardless of whether they be a Muslim or a person from the People of the Book [...]. This is the reported view of 'Ali, al-Nakhai', al-Shafi'i [38], Hammad, Ishaq and the people of Opinion [i.e. the Hanafi school]." [Ibn Qudamah, al-Mughni] .

b. **The Maliki and Shafi'i schools** do not see this as a condition, as the verse is clear in not making this a condition. The Qur'anic verse requiring *tasmiyyah* is directed to Muslims alone. Therefore any meat that religious scholars from the People of the book have stated as being lawful for their own congregation is lawful for our congregation.

> "This [i.e. tasmiyyah] is not a condition in relation to the People of the Book, as God has permitted us to partake in the meat of the People of the Book and He knows that there are those amongst them that leave out the tasmiyyah [...] nevertheless it is a requirement that they not mention the name of anything other than Him who they believe to be divine." [Al-Dardir, Sharh as-Saghir, v1, p314].

3.3 Tasmiyyah and machine slaughter

It should be pointed out from the outset that in Islamic law, it is not a condition that the slaughter be done by hand. Any sharp instrument in the control of a person that performs the act makes the meat lawful. However, for those who hold the *tasmiyyah* to be a condition of halal meat, there are a number of issues that make it questionable whether the condition of *tasmiyyah* is fulfilled. Taking poultry farming as an example:

3.3.1 Who is the slaughterer?
As the process is mechanical, the action in such cases is usually attributed to the one who operates the machine. In this case, this is merely the pushing of a switch at the start of each batch of slaughtering.

3.3.2 Repetition of tasmiyyah over each individual animal.
If a Muslim was to pronounce the name of God and switch on a machine used for mechanical slaughter, the first bird slaughtered may be halal, but the rest would remain unlawful for consumption, for it is a condition that each animal individually has the name of God pronounced over it. Although unintentional mistakes in this regard are overlooked, an intentional discrepancy leaves the meat unlawful.

> "The condition (for an animal to be halal) is that the animal is slaughtered straight after the pronouncement [of] the (tasmiyyah) before one begins doing something else. So much so that if a person laid down two sheep, one over the other, and slaughtered them simultaneously; pronouncing the name of God once, then they would both be halal, contrary to the situation where one slaughters them one after the other. The reason behind this is that the repetition of the act requires the repetition of the tasmiyyah." [Ibn Abidin, 6/402]

The above has also been mentioned in other schools of law, except that, as has preceded:

> "[T]he Shafi'i school do not make it a condition that one say the tasmiyyah, rather it is recommended, a position supported by Ibn Rushd [the grandfather], which is also one of the narrations from Ahmed.." [Mausuah', v21, 189-190]

3.3.3 Pronouncement of the tasmiyyah by an individual unconnected with the actual slaughter of the animal. This is where a person stands by the conveyer belt and pronounces the *tasmiyyah* while someone else controls the mechanics.

4. The severing of vital arteries.

Scholars have differed as to which parts of the neck need to be cut in the slaughter process. This is because there is no clear mention in religious texts of any particular veins/organs. All that is known is the practice

---

[38] As mentioned below, the position of the school of Imam al-Shafi is that it is not.

passed down from generation to generation, as well as what can be extrapolated linguistically from the words used in this context (such as *dhibh, nahr*, etc). The majority of the four veins must be cut with a knife, blade or any tool that is sharp and has a cutting edge. The four organs identified by scholars in this regard are [1] the wind pipe [*mari'i*] to the lungs [2] the oesophagus [*hulqum*] which goes to the stomach, and [3&4] the two jugular veins [*wadajan*].

The Shafi'i and Hanbali schools have held that if both of the first two are totally cut then the meat is lawful. The **Hanafi** school holds that three of the four need to be severed, while in the **Maliki** school, the whole of the oesophagus as well as the two jugular veins need to be cut for the animal to be halal. All agree that the place of slaughter is the throat and the upper part of the chest, specifically the four areas mentioned. [*Mausuah' al-Kuwaytiyyah, v24, pp177- 178*]

Whether this is attained through mechanical slaughter can only be verified through an actual inspection of abattoirs to ascertain whether the methods used do sever the minimum required arteries.[39]

5. That the animal be deemed alive at the time of slaughter.

It is known that the animals due to be slaughtered are pre-stunned. The issue that arises is whether electric stunning kills the animal before it is slaughtered, in which case the meat is unlawful. Also, there is the issue of whether it causes unnecessary pain to the animal, deeming it ethically questionable.

> *"...some experts insist that this [stunning] does reduce the animal's pain. If it is shown conclusively that this is indeed the case, and that the animal does not die from being stunned, then it is permissible to use these methods. Otherwise, it is not."* [Taqi Uthmani, pp83-84]

This can only be verified through research and in this regard, the Muslim World League set up a committee to look into the issues related to stunning.

6. Formal responses to the issue of stunning

6.1 The joint Muslim World League/World Health Organization meeting.

It recommended that *"If it could be shown that stunning with electric shock enabled the animal to die peacefully, then it would be Islamically lawful."*

The meeting also set up a committee of scholars of Islamic law and experts to study the effects of stunning, and to verify whether it: a) mitigates the slaughter process and does not constitute a form of torture; b) does not lead to death; and c) does not have any adverse effect on the animal nor cause harm to the consumer.

Findings.

The committee found that stunning: a) most probably mitigated the slaughter and eliminated pain; b) did not lead to death, provided that the conditions set out by the committee were met and c) had no adverse effects on the (meat of the) animal nor would it cause any harm to the consumer.[40]

---

[39] *The method of slaughter by machine devised by the Islamic Food and Nutrition Council of America and approved or accepted by Muslim countries varies from the machine slaughter method used in the industry in several ways as follows:*
[1] A Muslim, whilst pronouncing the name of God, switches on the machine [2] One Muslim slaughterman positions himself after the machine to make a cut on the neck, [as backup for] if the machine misses a bird or if the cut is not adequate for proper bleeding [3] In commercial poultry processing, generally the machine does not properly cut 5 to 10% of the birds. A Muslim then must cut these birds. [4] Height of the blade(s) must be adjusted to make a cut on the neck, right below the head, and not across the head or on the chest. The birds should be reasonably close in size to accomplish this requirement. [5] A rotary knife should be able to cut at least three of the passages in the neck. It is often difficult to accomplish this requirement with a single knife; hence a double knife set up may be required under such circumstances. [6] Any birds that are not properly cut may be tagged by the Muslim slaughterman/inspector, to be used as non-halal. [7] Two slaughtermen may be required to accomplish the above requirements, depending on the line speed and efficiency of the operation. The machine must be stopped during the breaks and must be restarted using the above procedure. "Regenstein & Chaudry, A Brief Introduction to Some of the Practical Aspects of the Kosher and Halal Laws for the Poultry Industry" [Edited by Alan R. Sams, p298]

[40] As per the research findings of Dr Muhammad Abdul Munim Abul Fadl, made between 15 and 25 November 1987, to the University of Edinburgh Faculty of Medicine, the Edinburgh abattoir and the Roslyn Poultry Research Centre. See *www.emro.who.int/publications/HealthEdReligion/Slaughter/index.htm]* The initial meeting was held at Jeddah during Rabi al-Awwal 1406 AH/December 1985)

Appendix

Text of the resolution of the Islamic fiqh council Jeddah N° 101/3/10 related to stunning

'ON SACRIFICIAL ANIMALS AND *SHARI'A* RULES FOR SLAUGHTERING THEM'

[...]

Fifth:

1. *Lawful slaughtering must, in principle, be carried out without knocking out the animal, since the Islamic method, by its requirements and rules, is the best because it is more merciful towards the animal and shortens its suffering. Therefore, it is requested from the concerned authorities to develop the means and tools to be used in slaughtering large animals, so as to fully comply with these requirements.*
2. *While complying with the provisions of here above paragraph 1, it is permitted to eat the meat of an animal slaughtered in a lawful way, after it is knocked out, when it is technically certified that the animal did not die from this operation before it is slaughtered. This procedure is defined as follows by experts :*

   a) Application of two electrodes on the temples or the forehead or the nape of the animal.
   b) The voltage must be between 100 and 400 volts.
   c) The electric power must be between 0,75 to 1 ampere for sheep and between 2 and 2,5 amperes for cattle.
   d) The electrical shock must last 3 to 6 seconds.
   e) It is prohibited to knock the animal out with a needle gun, an axe, a hammer or by inflating the animal as in the English method.
   f) It is prohibited to knock out poultry by electric shock, experience having demonstrated that in this method many animals die before they are slaughtered.
   g) It is allowed to eat the meat of an animal slaughtered after knocking it out with the use of a mixture of carbon dioxide and air or oxygen, or by using a round- headed pistol that would not provoke the death of the animal before it is slaughtered.

[The Council of the Islamic Fiqh Academy, holding its Tenth session in Jeddah, from 23 to 25 Safar 1418H (28 June to 3 July 1997)]

Lesson 5
Zakat case study - the scope of "in the path of God" (fisibilillah)

Lesson Five

Aim:
By the end of this lesson, students should be able to understand the issues related to giving Zakat funds outside the eight categories mentioned in the Qur'an and know whether zakat funds can be given to general causes such as mosques and hospitals.

Objectives:
By the end of this lesson, students should be able to display the ability to:
1. **Mention** what the phrase *fisibilillah* means.
2. **Outline** the meaning given to *fisibilillah* by the majority of scholars and what three proofs they base their view on.
3. **Mention** why some say that *fisibilillah* encompasses all acts of good without exception, and why this is considered a weak opinion by the majority of scholars.
4. **Explain** what is meant when this group say *'the eight categories are not mutually exclusive as they overlap.*
5. **Discuss** whether the Prophet ﷺ ever gave zakat funds outside the eight categories.
6. **Examine** the claim that some early Muslims allowed zakat to be used for communal projects.
7. **Explain** the case of those who say that zakat may be used outside the eight categories on the condition that it relates specifically to defending or promoting the faith of Islam.

1. The relevance of zakat in the modern age

Contemporary scholars have had to deal with a number of issues regarding the institution of zakat, many of which relate to the status and value of modern contracts and their usage in Islamic law. Another pressing issue that has been at the forefront of debate and research has been on the topic, what is considered a legitimate recipient of zakat?

This issue is connected to the question of whether or not zakat is primarily instituted to alleviate personal poverty in the Muslim community. Can it be used for capacity building in the Ummah, whether that be human or resource based, and so be utilized to serve the needs of the wider Muslim community and not just those traditionally in receipt of it?

Within the context of this discussion, the category of *fisibilillah* (in the path of God) has attracted growing interest. Classical scholars reached a consensus of sorts on what *fisibilillah* meant - namely financial aid that went to those engaged in defending the state from external aggression, thereby safeguarding the existence and influence of the Muslim faith on people's lives. Some also included those who travelled to perform Hajj. Can this class of recipient, in line with its general, literal meaning, be extended to include all types of good actions that are done in the service of Islam? More specifically, can Islamic institutions, mosques and other educational initiatives that seek to promote the Islamic message, come under this broad category?[41]

2. What is the meaning of *fisibilillah?*

There are three main positions on what *fisibilillah* refers to.

a. The classical understanding of the vast majority of legal scholars, as well as Qur'anic commentators. *Fisibilillah* is restricted to military expenditure for individual combatants in a legally sanctioned military scenario. Others also include those needy individuals travelling for Hajj as being part of this category as reported from Ibn Abbas and Ibn 'Umar.

b. Scholars that have sought to argue that *fisibilillah* is a term which refers to **all** categories of piety and goodness done for the sake of God, be they to help individuals or help in the structural promotion of a

---

[41] Note: This lesson is meant as a short survey of the issues involved. Due to the limited remit of this class, technical matters related to Arabic rhetoric and grammar, which make up the underlying area of research and contention in this issue, have only been mentioned in passing.

stronger Muslim community. Therefore, they would include initiatives such as hospitals, schools, road building projects, as well as other similar initiatives that aid the community.

c. Those scholars who have argued that *fisibilillah* cannot just be restricted to the definition given by earlier scholars (namely that of relating to the military meaning of the word). They argue that any initiative in keeping with the wider meaning of *jihad* - any activity that seeks to strengthen and promote the Islamic message and defend it from those antagonistic to its basic teachings is considered as *fisibilillah*, even if it is not overtly military.

2.1 The case of the majority

As this is the position of the overwhelming majority of scholars throughout Islamic history, there has been little attempt to explain or argue the case for such an interpretation. Unlike issues of Islamic law that were the subjects of protracted debate, this was one question in which the discussion revolved around details rather than any core disagreement.

The majority of scholars have restricted the meaning of *fisibilillah* to those engaged in military campaigns under the auspices of a legitimate Islamic leadership. They differ over details relating to this, such as whether it is a condition that the recipient be poor or not.[42]

They base this on the following:

2.1.1 The use of the term *fisibilillah* in the Shari'ah.

> "al-Sabil originally means 'the path', used grammatically for both the masculine and feminine form, the latter of which is more common. Sibil-Illah is a general term for all acts done with sincerity through which one intends to draw close to God through performing obligatory, supererogatory as well as other voluntary acts. If the term is used in no particular context, then it ostensibly refers to jihad, so much so that due to it being used so often as such, it is restricted to this meaning." [Ibn Athir, an-Nihayah, 2/338]

> "Lexically, the term 'fi-sibil-illah' means 'the way that leads to Him', may He be exalted, and it is often used to mean 'fighting for His cause', which may mean martyrdom that leads to pleasing God. The term was latterly applied to those who fight without [desire of]recompense, as they sacrifice more than regular paid soldiers and deserve to be given what helps them undertake this duty, even if they be rich." [Ibn Hajr al-Haithami, Tuhfat al-Muhtaj fi Sharh al Minhaj]

2.1.2 The restriction of the recipients to eight categories.

There would be no benefit in detailing and singling out all the groups of the recipients of zakat, only to then extend it to all types of good action. Such use of language would be deemed frivolous.

Imam al-Shafi'i said, commenting on the verse relating to the categories of zakat recipients *"and therefore God detailed precisely those deserving of zakat in His book, thereafter emphasizing this with his words **"a just portion from God"**. Therefore it is not for anybody to distribute charity in a way other than what God, may He be Exalted, has apportioned. These are the named categories that exist." [Ash-Shafi'i Al-Umm v2, p60].*

Ibn Qayyim al-Jawziyyah said: *"Divine wisdom dictates that wealth be distributed in a way that is just, and also fulfills the needs of the poor and destitute in such a way that they not require anything else. For this purpose, God obligated a portion of the wealth of the rich to be given to the poor to suffice them of want. In this way, injustice was repulsed from two sets of people: from the rich who would have refused to give what they should have; and second, from the one that receives it, [protecting him from] laying hands on what he or she does not deserve.*

In both cases, this would create great harm upon the [genuinely] poor and destitute, not to mention those in extreme poverty, leading them to trickery as well as extremes in seeking provisions. Therefore the Lord, may He be Exalted, took it upon Himself to distribute and apportion charity Himself, allocating it to eight categories encompassing two [broad] types of people:

---

[42] The *Maliki, Hanbali* and *Shafi'i* schools do not stipulate this as a requirement, while the *Hanafi* school do. The first three schools also allow funds to be channeled into the infrastructure needed for such engagement such as barracks etc.

- ***Those that take charity due to need*** in accordance with the immediacy, or otherwise, of their requirements, whether great or little. They are: the poor, the destitute, those seeking freedom from bondage, and the wayfarer.
- ***Those that take from the charity on account of their usefulness.*** They are the zakat collectors, those whose hearts are to be reconciled, those in debt on account of arbitrating between people, and those fighting in the way of God. Therefore, if the person taking zakat is not needy or provides no benefit to the community, they deserve no portion of zakat." [Zad al-Ma'ad, v1, p148].

2.1.3 There is no recorded precedence for a more general meaning amongst the Salaf.

Neither the earlier community, nor later scholars are reported as having been in the habit of allocating zakat funds to causes outside these eight categories, such as for general acts of piety and goodness. What is established is that they used to make use of other levies, sadaqah and charitable endowments (*waqf*), for such purposes.

2.2 The case of those that extend fisibilillah to all types of good

Certain authors have sought to prove that this category of *fisibillilah* is general in nature and should not be restricted to the classical understanding of jihad given to it by scholars, but rather extended to all types of good acts.

A representative of this view, Sadiq Hassan Khan, states *"As for fisibilillah, what is intended here is the path that leads to God, may He be Exalted; and jihad, even if it is the greatest of paths in the cause of God, there is no proof that this category is restricted only to this. Rather it is correct to designate this portion to whoever is on a path to God, may He be Exalted. This is [in accordance with] the linguistic meaning of the verse." [Al-Rawdah an-Nadiyyah, v1, p206].*

They base this on the following:

2.2.1 The original linguistic use of fisibillilah includes more than fighters.

One of the previous Shaykhs of al-Azhar, al-Shaltut said regarding *fisibillilah*, *'They are those general benefits which are not owned individually and also are not utilised by one specific group, but are owned by God, and their use and benefit is for God's creation.'*

He also says *"The word fisibilillah in the general sense is all things that protect and safeguard the material and spiritual status of the Ummah, and actualize the public face of this religion so that it is distinguished from others and through which it services its needs internally." [Al–Islam: Aqidah wa-ash-Shari'ah p124].*

The origin of this view lies in an understanding of the verse based on the original meaning of *fisibilillah*.
The eminent tafsir scholar *ar-Razi* mentioned the *Shafi'i* jurist *al-Qaffal* as having recorded that some unnamed jurists upheld the original linguistic meaning of *fisibilillah*. However, neither *al-Razi* nor *al-Qaffal* is reported to have personally held this position. The former was merely commenting on a possible linguistic reading of the verse which was adopted by some, while *al-Qaffal* was reporting the position of unnamed jurists.

Al-Razi said: *"One should know that the apparent meaning of fisibilillah does not necessarily imply a restriction on ghuzat (military personnel). For this reason, al-Qaffal, in his commentary of the verse, mentioned that some jurists allowed the use of sadaqah on all kinds of good deeds, such as funeral costs for the deceased, building fortifications and mosques, since fisibillilah [linguistically] covers all of these." [al-Razi, Tafsir al-Kabir].*

The quote of al-Razi was subsequently utilised by *al-Baqa'i* in his *Nadhm al-Durrar [8/506], Muhyuddin Shaykh Zad'ah* in his gloss of *Tafsir al-Baydawi [2/338] al-Alusi* in his *Tafsir Ruh al-Ma'ani [10/123]* as well as a number of other recent Qur'an commentators such as *Jamal-ad-Din Al-Qasimi [8/241].*

2.2.1.1 Analysis

A survey of the Qur'anic use of *fisibilillah* (with the preposition *fi*) shows that it is in line with the interpretation that the majority have given it. *"What comes to mind in relation to Sibilillah is that it refers to military actions and the majority of what appears in the noble Quran is of this sort." [al-Nawawi, al-Majmu', 6/212]*

2.2.1.2 Analysis

The basic wisdom of zakat, as mentioned by Ibn Qayyim above, is to focus a specific type of charity to well defined categories of recipients. The opinion that seeks to give *fisibilillah* a general meaning of all acts of goodness and piety would defeat this wisdom by dispersing the limited amount of wealth collected by zakat over a wide and desperate group of people.

Even *Rashid Rida,* who promoted a more expansive understanding of *fisibilillah* stated *"This generalization has not been stated by anyone amongst the Salaf, nor those that came after them amongst the scholars."* *[Tafsir al-Manar, v10, p503]*

2.2.2 The eight categories are not mutually exclusive since they overlap.

Four of the categories, namely the poor; the destitute; those seeking freedom from bondage; and the wayfarer; are given zakat funds based on the existence of poverty. Therefore, the list of eight is merely a rhetorical device used to emphasise a general quality that exists in the recipients of zakat, rather than an exhaustive list seeking to restrict those to whom zakat can be distributed. This is further proven by the fact that both the words *faqir* and *miskin* are used interchangeably.

2.2.2.1 Analysis
God specifically singled out eight categories in the verse on zakat. Permitting zakat to be used for causes that operate for the general good of the community would negate the benefit of singling out such categories. Ibn Qudamah al-Hanbali, in the context of talking about the permissibility or otherwise of using zakat to build bridges and roads, said *"The grammatical particle 'innama' is used [in Arabic] to indicate restriction by establishing the ruling for what is mentioned, thereby negating everything other than what is referred to. It is constructed of two [linguistic] particles, one negative and the other affirmative. Therefore, this is similar to the words of God "Indeed God is the one true God" [An-Nisa:171] meaning there is no god except God, and also His words "Indeed you are a warner." [Ra'd:7] meaning you are nothing other than a warner." [al-Mughni, 6/420].*

With regard to the interchangeability of *faqir* and *miskin,* a general rule about these types of word pairings is said to be that *"If they are used together, they differ in meaning, but when used individually they have the same import" [idha ijtama'aa ikhtalafaa, wa idha ikhtalifaa ijtma'aa].* Therefore if they are used in the same text they have to donate different things, as with the verse on zakat recipients.

2.2.2.2 Analysis
The meaning given to *fisibilillah* by those that seek a general meaning to the words would include the other seven categories also mentioned in the zakat verse, thereby defeating the whole wisdom of individually mentioning them as those deserving of zakat. This goes against the basic rules of eloquent speech.

2.2.3 The Prophet ﷺ reportedly gave zakat funds to other than the eight categories for the general good of the community.

The core proof used by this group of writers is from the Prophetic sunnah, namely in an instance where a group of the *Ansar* went to the area of *Khaybar* and later found one of their group to have been murdered. They accused the tribe who lived where he was found of having committed the murder, but they had no proof of this, and the tribe denied any involvement. The Prophet ﷺ, in view of the danger of a protracted conflict arising from the dispute, gave camels as blood money (*diya'*) to the family of the murdered man. What is claimed is that this was from camels that were part of the zakat funds. As blood money (*diya'*) does not come under any of the categories of eight zakat recipients, it has been taken as a precedent for using zakat funds for other than the eight categories mentioned in *Surah Tawbah.* Once this precedence is established, it points to the easing in the restrictions on who can be deemed a legitimate recipient of zakat.

However, the conflicting details of this instance leave a question mark over this view. This is reflected in the various narrations of the hadith *matn* itself, some of which are mentioned below.

2.2.3.1 Analysis of *the different narrations of the matn of the hadith in question.*
Ibn Hajr in his commentary on Sahih al-Bukhari *(hadith 6898)* commented on the different narrations of the incident:

> *"Some have claimed that this wording ['from the camels of sadaqah'] is a mistake on the part of the narrator Sa'id ibn Ubayd, because Yahya ibn Sa'id specifically mentions [the words] 'from his own [wealth] (min 'indihi).' Some have attempted to make the two narrations conform to each other by saying that the Prophet ﷺ bought the camels and then gave them from himself [in a personal capacity], or that the meaning of 'from his own [wealth]' is from the general treasury (bayt al-mal), which is kept aside for public benefit. The word 'charity' (sadaqah) was used to describe this only in as much as sadaqah could be*

used freely to bring to [an] end disputes and heal tensions. Some have taken the words literally. Qadi 'Iyad makes mention of some scholars who permitted the use of zakat monies for general projects (al-masalih al-'amm).'" [Ibn Hajar, Fath al-Bari, v12, p292]

These narrations provide conflicting information as to the circumstances in which the Prophet ﷺ paid the wealth, as well as the source from which he paid it.

2.2.3.2 Analysis: *How do most scholars explain the hadith?*
Scholars generally agree that if it is not possible to make all narrations mutually compatible (*tawfiq*) then it is better to choose the version that is in line with the majority of narrators, as well as agreeing with any relevant general principle of hadith or law. The general principle here is that it is not permitted to give the *diya'* (blood money) from zakat funds. Based on this, many scholars have criticised the specific wording of the hadith narrator *"from the camels of sadaqah (i.e. zakat)."*

Al-Nawawi, after giving a number of different explanations to the incident, said "The majority of our Companions (i.e. from the Shafi'i school), as well as others, have said [that] it means that he ﷺ bought them [the camels] from people who had received them as sadaqah - after they took ownership of them. He ﷺ then gave it voluntarily to the family of the person killed [...]. The preferred opinion is that which we have related from the majority of scholars, namely that he bought them from the camels of zakat." [al-Nawawi, Sharh Muslim, v11, p148, hadith no.1669]

"The narration that states 'from his own wealth' is more correct than that which states 'from the camels of sadaqah'." [ibn Hajar, Fath al-Bari, v12, p292]

2.2.3.3 Analysis
The hadith text mentioned has no indication of its support for the position that zakat can be used for the general welfare and interest of the community, as the blood money paid was not just for a general interest relating to the community, but rather was for a particular interest - for the family receiving it. The underlying reason for the Prophet ﷺ having paid the blood money was to appease and satisfy the family and relatives of the murdered individual. The other point is that this was most probably not given from zakat funds. Most importantly, if it was permitted for funds to be used in this way, we would have had more reported instances of this from the sunnah, the actions of the *'four Khulafa'* and the *Salaf*.

This last point leads us on to some reports that seem to indicate the permissibility of using zakat for general community welfare.

2.2.4 Some of the *Salaf* allowed zakat funds to be used for common projects such as constructing bridges and roads.

They take as proof for this what is related from Anas ibn Malik and al-Hasan al-Basri, that they both permitted zakat to be used for the construction of bridges as well as roads. *[See Ibn Qudamah, al-Mughni]*

2.2.4.1 Analysis
This opinion seems to be misrepresented, as what they permitted was not the use of zakat funds for constructing the aforementioned: rather what they were referring to was taxes paid to government officials at checkpoints set out on roads and bridges taken from passing merchants. The question was therefore: could this be considered as zakat in reference to the person paying it? Their opinion was that it could be. However, the majority of scholars consider such taxation to not absolve one of paying one's zakat.

2.3 The case of those that extend fisibilillah to include all forms of promoting Islam.

This group of contemporary scholars has advocated a more balanced approach to the meaning of *fisibillilah* than the previous group above, while at the same time arguing for a wider meaning to be given to *jihad* than that given to it by the majority. Whilst they agree with the majority that *fisibilillah* is used in the verse to convey the meaning of *jihad*, they argue that as times have changed, the most effective manner in which zakat allocated to this category can be used is through initiatives that help promote and safeguard the faith in areas where it is vulnerable to attack.

They argue that the present state of the Muslim Ummah is such that it has become necessary to advance financial aid to a wider array of recipients, particularly those in non-Muslim lands where there is little other financial support available to repulse harm from Muslims. This means that scholars should reexamine the issue to consider whether there is any room for more leniency in the interpretation given to the issue at hand.

It is important to point out that the arguments used by this group are generally the same as those used by the previous group, and any responses to these from the majority of scholars are as have preceded in relation to position two. The main divergence between the latter two positions is that this group holds that the term *fisibilillah* is used in legal texts ostensibly for *jihad* and not for all types of good actions. They do, however, give a wider meaning to *jihad* than that given by the majority.

One of the main proponents of this point of view – Sh. Yusuf al-Qardawi, provided some examples of where such funds could be used:

> "[B]uilding centers for the call to Islam (da'wah) which provide correct and sound Islamic information [...].
>
> Another example is the establishment of a purely 'Islamic' newspaper, which would provide guidance to Muslim men and woman in their daily lives and lead to Islamic political and social awareness [...] printing Islamic books is yet another area where jihad in the way of God can be practiced, for it is crucial to reveal the treasures of this religion as a better way of life. Yet another example of jihad is to support full-time workers in the way of God. These and similar activities deserve the share of zakah for the sake of God." [al-Qardawi, Fiqh az-Zakat, 2/669]

3. General observations on the third position

Whilst the general thrust of the argument to broaden the use of zakat funds seems to be appealing, due to the scarcity of *waqf* and charitable endowments since the fall of the Caliphate, there are a still number of outstanding practical issues that, from a *shari'ah* perspective, require attention for this last position to be actionable. They mostly relate to safeguarding zakat funds from being used subjectively and arbitrarily.

1. **A clear demarcation between sadaqah and zakat has to be maintained**. These are clearly two different types of charity with separate temporal as well as spiritual benefits. While no one denies the importance of many educational and religious initiatives, such projects have always been financially supported by individuals through endowments and voluntary charity. This is one of the reasons why the reward for voluntary charity is far greater; it is given to all good causes at the discretion of the giver.

2. **That such funds be focused on initiatives of importance comparable to *jihad* in terms of the viability and preservation of the Muslim faith.** As such funds are earmarked for *fisibilillah* in as much as it means *jihad*, the critical nature of such projects would need to be comparable to the original agreed upon expenditure for *fisibilillah*. In other words it should relate to a demonstrable struggle to protect the faith.

3. **For those living in majority non-Muslim countries, they would need to ascertain whether the resources that they have available for religious projects are lacking, or comparable to those available to their brethren in Muslim lands.** One of the points made in the West is that the Muslim community lack sufficient funds to ensure its continual presence there, and so it should be given the right to make use of zakat funds for community projects as an exceptional ruling. Given the relative affluence in which they live, it is essential to justify zakat funds being used for projects whose suitability is disputed. Are the conditions that Muslims live in more dire than those faced by Muslim communities in the past or even in the Muslim world presently, that such unprecedented steps in zakat allocation should be undertaken?

4. **That such funds are not used for sectarian or personal projects associated with those collecting the zakat**. This is arguably the greatest danger in the misuse of zakat funds. Echoing this problem, even Sh. Rashid Rida says *"If this affair of earmarking zakat to any type of pious action was given over to the authorities and leaders, they would distribute it in accordance with their personal preferences in a way that would negate the wisdom of imposing zakat on those that pay it."* [Tafsir al-Manar, v10, p504].

5. **The imperative to independently verify individual project suitability.** The lack of an adequately informed leadership that transparently verifies those causes that would fulfill the requirements of *fisibilillah* means that individuals giving zakat to such causes would need to ascertain for themselves the suitability of such projects for zakat funds. If they do not qualify for such help, the zakat given will not have been deemed as having been properly paid, thereby leaving an essential, religious obligation as not having been performed.

Lesson 6
The Ethics of war and the contemporary issue of Suicide bombings

Lesson Six

Aim: By the end of this lesson students should be able to understand the issues related to the modern military tactic of suicide bombing.

Objectives:
By the end of this lesson the student should be able to display the ability to:
1. **Assess** the background to *'The Just War'* theory.
2. **Explain** why there are different Arabic terms used for what is referred to as *'suicide bombing'*.
3. **Outline** what the importance of legitimate leadership and the status of noncombatants has when looking at this issue.
4. **Mention and analyze** the *quranic* proofs put forward by those that support such actions.
5. **Mention and analyze** the proofs from the Sunnah put forward by those that support such actions.
6. **Explain and analyze** the philosophical proof of those that support such actions, outlining the drawbacks of such reasoning.
7. **Explain** what is meant by *'shahid'* and why this is of relevance to the status of one that carries out *'suicide bombing.'*

> *"And fight in the path of God those who fight you: but do not commit excesses, for God does not love those who exceed the bounds."* [2:190]

> *Samurah ibn Jundub narrates that "The Messenger 🕊 used to encourage the giving of charity and forbade Muthla (mutilation)."* [Abu Daud]

1. The Just War

One of the things that has given the Islamic faith its historical resilience is that it addressed the root of every major moral issue that faces humankind. Whether it be in-depth legislation on divorce law, the ethics of just trade, and the scourge of racism, the religious sources are anything but silent in offering advice and, where necessary, legislation to ensure that human interaction is built fairness, balance, and equity.

A case in point is the issue of conflict and war. The legitimacy of using force of arms is something that every civilization has had to grapple with. Who decides when war is justified and what type of force is permitted? These questions were in the past left to the discretion of military leaders, rather than philosophers and thinkers. The theory of *"The Just War"* and the associated issues on the rules of engagement came about in a large part to curtail the excesses committed on the battlefield. Under this theory, the conditions for warfare being ethically justified were that it be conducted under the auspices of an authority vested with a mandate to use force; that this be undertaken with due care to proportionality and that the actions undertaken be in the service of a just cause. It should be pointed out that the Islamic faith and the extensive legal tradition set down clear rules on the ethics of war well before such norms were recognized in the West.

As the *shari'ah* is ostensibly a religious code of law, any contravention of the laws by Muslims is held to be not just crimes against man but also a mortal sin against God. Therefore any armed conflict, for it to be ethical, has to adhere to strict laws of engagement under the auspices of a legitimate authority. Otherwise any action, however well intentioned, stands condemned in religious law.

2. Contextual considerations - Leadership & Noncombatants

For the issue referred to as *'suicide bombing'* to be adequately addressed from the perspective of Islamic law, the term needs to be properly defined so that any associated issues that have a bearing on arriving at an informed ruling may be addressed. There are three distinct components that are of relevance. Two of these, though not related to the assessment of the ethical legitimacy of the act itself, are integral to it from a practical and operational perspective and so important in the contextualization of the phenomena.

As the current phenomena of *'suicide bombing'* has appeared within a vacuum of authority, the **first** issue relates to verifying the existence of **legitimate leadership** that authorize such acts.
The **second** issue relates to the targeting of **noncombatants** in suicide bombing as a means of achieving specific aims. These two components will only be dealt with in summary form.

The **third** component, that of the act itself, involves an analysis of the nature of **'suicide attacks'** from the perspective of the status of one carrying them out in the eyes of Islamic Jurisprudence (*fiqh*).

2.1 Legitimate leadership

Even a cursory look at classical '*Siyar*'[43] literature points clearly to the fact that military action in Islamic law is conditional upon it being undertaken by an acknowledged ruler or state. It is also understood that the enemy is another well defined state and that the declaration of war has been given clearly after having exhausted all other channels of engagement. There is also a consensus that if an opposing army attacks it is an obligation on each individual to defend their lives and property.

However non-state activity in effect undermines legitimate state structures and so is classified in Islamic law as tantamount to insurrection (*baghi*) against the state. Insurrection in this instance can be defined as rising up against the legitimate Muslim ruler or denying the ruler the prerogative of deciding on the military activity of the state. By scholarly consensus, those that head such insurrections against the ruler are to be fought. *[al-Dasuqi, Hashiyyah, v4, pg 460].*

> "The question of declaring war (or not) is entrusted to the executive authority [...]. Decisions of this kind for each Muslim state, such as those questions dealing with ceasefire ['aqd al-hudna], peace settlement ['aqd al-amân] and the judgment on prisoners of war [al-ikhtâr fi asîr] can only be dealt with by the executive or political authority [imâm] or by a subordinate authority appointed by the former authority [amîr mansûbin min jihati l-imâm].
> This is something Muslims take for granted from the authority of our naql [scriptures] such that none will reject it except those who betray their 'aql [intellect]. The most basic legal reason ['illa aslîyya] is that this matter is one that involves the public interest, and thus consideration of it belongs solely to the authority." [Defending the Transgressed, Sh. Afifi, in 'The State we are in', Pg 128] [44]

2.2 Noncombatants

> "Abu Bakr gave ten directives to his commander in greater Syria "I council you with ten [things]: Do not kill women or children or an aged, infirm person. Do not cut down fruit-bearing trees. Do not destroy a place that may be inhabited. Do not slaughter sheep or camels except for food. Do not burn hives or scatter their inhabitants. Do not steal from the booty, and do not be cowardly." [Malik, Muwatta, Bab nahi 'an Qatl a-Nisa]

The strict prohibition on the killing of noncombatants in a state of war is known to be one of the essentials of this religion (*ma'lum bi-darurah*). Any intentional act that targets and kills noncombatants is tantamount to the killing of the whole of humanity.

Related to the issue of noncombatants is the issue of what type of weapons may be used in war. Weapons of mass destruction are highly reprehensible in Islamic law precisely because they kill indiscriminately, and it is only permitted for a State to posses such armaments in cases of necessity as a means of achieving parity with an opposing force. The principle of reciprocity (*mu'amala bil-mithl*) comes into play in Islamic law in such cases if no other option is deemed feasible. *[Ibn Qudamah, al-Mughni, v8 pg 448-9]*

> "The original ruling [al-asl] for using a bomb (the medieval precedents: Greek fire [qitâl bil-nâr or ramy al-naft] and catapults [manjanîq]) as a weapon is that it is makrûh [offensive] because it kills indiscriminately [ya'ummu man yuqâtilû wa-man lâ yuqâtilû], as opposed to using rifles (medieval example: a single bow and arrow). If the indiscriminate weapon is used in a place where there are civilians, it becomes harâm except when used as a last resort [min darûra] (and of course, by those military personnel authorized to do so)." [Defending the Transgressed, Sh. Afifi, in 'The State we are in', Pg 134]

---

[43] The area of Islamic law dealing with war and interstate relations.

[44] "Ibn Qudamah (d.1223) and others add that a ruler is one whose leadership (imamate) has been confirmed through a pledge of allegiance, designation by his predecessor, or the conquering of territory. With regards to the acquisition of power, it should also be noted that the definition of "ruler" might also apply to someone who seizes power through a military coup. In this case, two stipulations apply, in which the ruler (1) implements measures to ensure public security; if he cannot accomplish this, he does not qualify as a legitimate ruler, even if he conquered his opponents and (2), he does not openly encourage acts of disbelief, unless of course he states openly his own disbelief. If these two stipulations are met, then he should be treated as a legitimate Muslim ruler." [Ibn Bayyah, The Culture of Terrorism, pg 12]

The ruling prohibiting the targeting of noncombatants as well as the use of indiscriminate weaponry is one that has the backing of scholarly consensus. It should also be mentioned that the categories afforded safety in the hadith above who then take up arms on a battle field forfeit the safety afforded to them on account of becoming active combatants. *[Ibn Qudamah, al-Mughni, v 8, pg 477]*

3. 'Suicide attacks'

> *"Do not kill yourselves. Verily, God is merciful to you. And, whoever does that, out of animosity and wrongfully, We shall burn him in a Fire. And that is easy for God." [4:29-30]*

> *"Whoever strangles himself will be strangling himself in the Fire, and whoever stabs himself will be stabbing himself in the Fire." [Bukhari, 1365]*

> *"Among those before you, there was a man with a wound, and in anguish, he took a knife and cut his hands, and the blood did not stop until he died. God said, "My servant has hastened the ending of his life, so I have prohibited Heaven to him." [Bukhari, 3463]*

3.1 Modern dilemmas? The contemporary nature of suicide bombings

While Islamic scholarship has extensive literature on all aspects of war, one issue that has not been covered is the case of what is termed *'suicide bombings'*. This is due to the fact it was never used as a tactic of war within Sunni Islam until the 1990's.

3.2 Definitions and terms

3.2.1 Definition : *Suicide bombings can be defined as an attack designed to kill others where the death of the attacker is a necessary component of the action. The attack is accomplished through one's death and the use of one's body as a weapon.*

The permissibility or otherwise of such an act can only be looked into once the previous two conditions have been fulfilled [1] That this be in a war situation under the direct command of a legitimate leadership against a well defined enemy. [2] That noncombatants are not targeted. Non-state vigilantism using indiscriminate tactics to kill indiscriminately is therefore clearly *haram*.

3.2.2 Terms: There are a number of terms used by different people defining such actions.

a. *'Amaliyyah Intihariyyah.*   An act through which one commits suicide while attacking others.
b. *'Amaliyyah Fida'iyyah.*   An act were one sacrifices one's life for a higher cause.
c. *'Amaliyyah Istishhadiyyah.* An act which one preempts becoming a *'shahid'* (martyr).

As *'suicide bombing'* is a modern phenomena, none of these terms exist in classical Islamic law. A large part of the discussion around this topic hinges on the search for suitable precedences that correspond to the topic at hand. If the conditions above are met and such an activity is contemplated as a military tactic, then is the act itself permitted? What are the proofs or precedences for such actions?

3.3 The proofs

There are three main types of proofs produced by those that support such acts.

1. Quranic evidence.
2. Hadith evidence
3. Philosophical evidence

3.3.1 Quranic evidence.

The most oft-quoted Quranic 'proof' for *'suicide bombing'* is the story of the people of the trenches mentioned in *Sura al-Buruj*. In the story we find a king who has tried various means to kill a young boy who is challenging his authority and calling him to the belief in the one true God. Every time he tries to take the boy's life he fails. The boy in the story then indicates the only way that this could be done. For those that claim *'suicide bombing'* is permitted, the story shows that sacrificing one's life for the sake of one's faith is legitimate, and not considered suicide.

> *"You will not be able to kill me until [...] you gather the people on a plateau, hang me on a palm-trunk, take an arrow from my quiver, place it in the bow, and say, 'In the name of God, the Lord of the boy' and shoot me." The king did this, and thereby managed to kill the boy as predicted, but the people who had gathered began saying, "We believe in God, the*

> *Lord of the boy!" The king ordered trenches to be dug, fires lit in them, and for the people to be thrown into them if they refused to give up their faith. This was done, and eventually a woman was brought with her infant, and she hesitated to jump because of the child [in her arms]. It said "Mother! Remain patient for you are upon the truth." [Muslim]*

3.3.1.1 Text Analysis:

- The example gives no support to the issue at hand because the one killing the boy is the king and not the boy himself. *'Suicide bombing'* is defined as an attack designed to kill others where the death of the attacker is a necessary and premeditated part of the action. The attack is therefore accomplished through one's death and the use of one's body as a weapon. Suicide defined as when the killer (*qatil*) and the killed (*maqtul*) are the same.
- Scholars have differed over whether, in an issue where we do not have a clear ruling in our own Islamic religious text, the law for previous nations *(shar' man qablana)* which is narrated in the hadith sets a valid precedence for Muslims.

3.3.2 Hadith evidence

There are numerous reports used by supporters of *'suicide bombing'* and they all relate to one particular action: where an individual throws caution to the wind and single-handedly attacks a far superior army *(inghimas fil 'aduw)* immersing himself into the enemy. This is agreed by all scholars to be not only permitted but indeed praiseworthy in a war situation. Is this the *'classical precedent'* for *'suicide bombing'* which can be the basis for an analogy to prove the praiseworthy nature of such acts? These hadith are also the main argument produced by supporters of *'suicide bombing'*. Mention will only be made of a few of these as they all point to the same scenario.

> *Mu'adh ibn 'Afra' asked the Messenger of God ﷺ "What makes God laugh upon His slave? He said   "Immersing himself into the enemy without armor.' Mu'adh then took off his armor and fought until he was killed." [Ibn Abi Shaybah, Musannaf, v5, pg 338]*

> *"Neither Abu Ayyub al-Ansari nor Abu Musa al-Ash`ari criticized a man plunging alone into a raging army and remaining steadfast until he was killed [...] It has been authentically reported that a companion asked the Messenger of God ﷺ about what makes God laugh upon a servant, and he ﷺ said, "His immersing himself into the enemy without armor", whereupon the man removed his armor and entered the enemy [ranks, fighting] until he was killed." [Ibn Hazm, Al-Muhalla, v7, pg 294]*

3.3.2.1 Text Analysis:

- The hadith reports are dissimilar to the issue at hand and so constitute what is termed in legal methodology as an analogy which is based on a faulty premise (*qiyas ma' al-fariq*). This is because the person who immerses himself into the midst of the enemy lines is (a) not premeditating his own death and (b) not using the destruction of his or her own body as the weapon thereby inevitably taking their own life in the process.
- One of the most foundational legal principles in Islamic law is that actions are ascribed to those that perform them. Taking one's own life in a premeditated manner, such as strapping explosives to one's body, even with an intention of achieving a higher motive, is of no consequence in changing the act from being one of suicide.
- In the hadith literature, the person is always killed by the enemy, whereas suicide is defined as death where the killer (*qatil*) and the killed (*maqtul*) are the same. The fact that the person is killed by their own hands is admitted by those that support such acts and is acknowledged to be a problem.

> *"Having established the permissibility of plunging into the enemy and attacking alone even when death is certain, we continue and say that the martyrdom operations are derived from this principle. There is one difference between the martyrdom operations and their classical precedent, namely that in our case the person is killed by his own hand, whereas in the other he was killed by the enemy. We also explain that this difference does not affect the verdict."   [Al-'Ayyiri, The Islamic Ruling on the Permissibility of Martyrdom Operations']*

However, having promised to explain this anomaly, the author of the document fails to explain how this difference between the two scenarios does not change the verdict.

3.3.3 Philosophical evidence

The gist of this argument is that even though taking one's life goes against the law of God because of it being a betrayal of the trust of life given to us by God, we are permitted to forfeit this trust if it is as an act of altruism *(ithaar)* and sacrifice for the benefit of others.

One of the writers on this topic takes his proof from the writings of the famous legal philosopher al-Shatibi who in his book *'al-Muwafaqat'* discusses, amongst other things, the rights that God has over human beings. Al-Shatibi states that the life and body of an individual belong to God and is a trust which may only be used in a way that is in conformity with God's law. The Islamic prohibition on suicide is clearly understood to stem from this. However the author seeks to justify a person sacrificing their own life if it is for the greater good *(al-maslaha al-'amma)*.

> *"The desire should not be to give away their life, but rather the person's intention should be directed towards strengthening religion and protecting it from the enemy that is being ambushed. At the same time he should be pleased to sacrifice his soul in this cause if the need arises. This is the meaning of the words of Al-Shatibi:*
>
> *"It is not permitted to gain closeness to God through a difficulty in and of itself. One can only draw close to God through difficult acts that are permitted."*
>
> *From this point of view we come to know that the suicide groups which gamble with their lives in the path of God are perfectly allowed to practice this action without any religious reprimand and without falling into the sin of having committed suicide if the aim of the person that commits the suicide is simply to aid in weakening the enemy. This, together with his hope and certainty of God's Mercy and Bounty that he be spared by the miracle of protection from the normal course of death. However, this cannot happen except through true faith in God." [al-Buti, al-Qadaya al-Mu'asirah, v2, pg 155-6]*

3.3.3.1 Text Analysis:

This is the most principled approach to the issue at hand. However it raises a number of further questions:

- **Intentions 1**. If acts carried out in warfare are only judged by intentions independent of the laws that govern war, how will it be possible to have objective guidelines on what is and is not permitted? Is the only thing of relevance that the person performing the act thinks and intends it to be justified regardless of what the religious texts agree upon? This idiosyncrasy is pointed out by Hafez in his article on the topic:

> *"It is remarkable to note the self-interested and contradictory ways Jihadi Salafists employ and dismiss the notion of human intentionality. In the case of killing fellow Muslims, those deemed 'apostates' are killed regardless of their intensions or reasons for their conduct. The intentions behind their actions are dismissed as irrelevant as long as their manifest conduct appears to be in violation of major Islamic principles. In the case of suicide bombings, however, the outward appearance of violating major Islamic principles against self-immolation is treated as secondary to the intention of the bombers. It does not matter that the suicide bomber is killing himself, as long as his intention is to raise God's word on earth. This shifting methodology clearly reflects the tendentious nature of Jihadi Salafist interpretations of the Islamic tradition." [Hafez, The Alchemy of Martyrdom: Jihadi Salafism and Debates over Suicide Bombings in the Muslim World,Asian Journal of Social Science 38 (2010) 364–378]*

- **Intentions 2**. One of the basic legal principles in Islam is that **acts are ascribed to those that perform them**. Therefore, the *intention* that one may have for taking one's own life is of no consequence in changing the act from being one of suicide.

- **Limits of altruism (*ithaar*).** There is no definitive link between altruism *(ithaar)*, sacrifice for others (which is permitted and even recommended in a war situation), and the premeditated ending of one's own life. The law has clearly put down limits regarding allowable acts of sacrifice. In this context it is the law that judges whether an act is commendable or not. As al-Shatibi himself states:

> *"The preservation of one's life, perfecting one's intellect and body are from the rights that God has over mankind and not from the rights of Man per se [...]. It is God that nurtures and perfects a person's life, body and intellect and it is through this they attain what they have. It is not allowed for the individual to forfeit [life]." [al-Shatibi, al-Muwafaqat, v2, pg 373].*

- **Legal value is given to actions based on the laws on nature.** The author appears to concede that the death of the one undertaking this act is through their own actions and therefore tantamount to killing oneself in a premeditated manner (i.e. suicide). However he makes the legality of the act dependent upon the hope and intention that the laws of nature will miraculously change to allow one to survive, thereby preventing inevitable suicide. It is therefore acknowledged that the act will be suicidal unless the laws of nature are prevented from running their course by a divine miracle!

4. Who is a Shahid? [45]

> "Do not think of those who have been killed in the cause of God as dead. Rather, they are alive with their Lord, being given provision." [3:169]

A person killed in battle is given a special title, that of a 'shahid'. The author of "The Islamic Ruling on the Permissibility of Martyrdom Operations"[46] seeks to prove the legitimacy of 'suicide bombing' through a misreading of Islamic legal texts that when read as they should be, lead to a conclusion opposite that arrived at by the author.

One example of this centres on the discussion within *fiqh* literature when considering a martyr (*shahid*) [47]. All such sources indicate that a person that plans and carries out an act where they will be the agent of their own death cannot be considered a martyr. The reason for this is simple. The texts conclusively show that legal scholars did not consider intentionality when deciding on who is considered a 'shahid'. In other words they do not look at intentions independent of the laws that govern war as mentioned before. They instead focused on the objective criteria of modality and agency of death. The use of such texts in support of 'suicide bombing' is at the very least a disingenuous use of the Islamic legal sources.

4.1 The Schools of law on who is a Shahid

4.1.1 The Maliki school

> "A person killed while fighting warring unbelievers, even if in Islamic lands, such as if the enemy attacked the Muslims, [is a martyr]. [This is the case] even if he did not engage in fighting on account of being unaware or asleep, or is killed by a Muslim who mistook him for an enemy, trampled by a horse, **mistakenly** smitten by his own sword or arrow, or by having fallen into a well or from a cliff during the fighting." [Dardir, Al-Sharh al-Kabir, v1, pg 666]

4.1.2 The Shafi'i school

> 'The shahid is a person that dies fighting the enemy as a result of the fighting itself (man mata fi qital al-kuffar bi sababihi), regardless of whether he is killed by the enemy, dies as a result of being hit by a Muslim weapon by mistake, or [when] his own weapon **came back upon himself** and he died." [al-Shurbini, Mughni al-Muhtaj, v1, pg 520]

> 'One who is killed while engaged with the enemy is a shahid. If the fighter's weapon **came back upon himself** and he died or he is hit by mistake from the weapon of a Muslim he is [also] a shahid as is unanimously held by the scholars [of the school]." [al-Juwayni, al-Nihayyah, v3 (20), pg 35]

4.1.3 The Hanbali school

> "If the person is killed **by his own weapon falling back on himself, then he is like the person killed by the enemy [...].** However if he has fallen off his mount or is found dead without any apparent signs [of injury], then he is to be washed. [Ibn Qudamah, al-Mughni, v3, pg 473-4]

---

[45] *Why the martyr is called a witness (shahid):*(1) Because God and the Prophet have testified concerning his entry into Heaven; (2) Because he is alive before his Lord; (3) Because the angels of mercy witness the taking of his soul; (4) Because he will be among those who testify over nations on the Day of Resurrection; (5) Because his faith and good ending have outwardly been witnessed; (6) Because he has a witness to his death, namely his blood; (7) Because his soul immediately witnesses Heaven. [See Nawawi, Sharh Sahih Muslim, 1/515, Al-Majmu', 1/277]

[46] Most probably penned by Yusuf al-'Ayyiri, the former Saudi Arabian leader of al-Qa`ida.

[47] In the fiqh literature, there is a consensus that the *shahid* is not to be washed before burial but differ on whether they should have the funeral prayer prayed on them. The imams Malik, al-Shafi'i and Ahmed state that they are not to be prayed on, while another narration from Ahmed and the position of Abu Hanifa is that the funeral prayer should be said on them. *[Ibn Qudamah, al-Mughni, v3, pg 467]*

4.1.4 The Hanafi school

"Anyone who is killed while fighting pagans (mushrikin), rebels (bughat), or brigands (harbi), by a means attributed to the enemy, whether directly or consequentially, is a martyr (shahid). ***Anyone who is killed by a means not specifically attributed to [an action of] the enemy is not considered a martyr."*** *[Zaylai, Tabyin al-Haqa'iq, v1/247, Al-Bahr al-Ra'iq, v2/211]*

"Therefore if a person is killed by a stray unmanned horse from the enemy side, an animal from the Muslim side, a stray arrow targeted at the enemy that strikes him, or the Muslim army flees from the enemy thereby pushing him into a ditch or fire and he dies, he will not die as a shahid in contradistinction to the view of Abu Yusuf. This is because all these scenarios break any connection the death may have had to the actions of the enemy." [Ibn Abidin, al-Hashiyyah, v2, pg 249]

Text Analysis:

The four schools of Sunni law specifically rule out considering one that *intentionally* causes their own death in battle as a martyr. Moreover the Hanafi school states that only the person whose death was directly caused by an intentional act of the enemy is treated as a *shahid* for the laws relating to martyrs. The remaining three schools only consider one who *unintentionally* or *mistakenly* ends up causing their own death as a martyr.

Therefore one can conclusively state that when deciding one who is treated as a martyr:

[a] Muslim scholars did not take intentionality into consideration.
[2] The criteria of modality and agency of death are to be investigated when deciding on who is treated as a martyr, as these are the only objective measures to ascertain intention.

Towards a Tranquil Soul 2

The Spiritual Ailments of the Heart and their Cures

Module Tzk 2.05.D

iSyllabus
islam · iman · ihsan

Lesson One
The two sources of spiritual ailments and heedlessness

> **Lesson One:**
> **Aim:** By the end of this lesson, the students should appreciate the two different sources of the ailments of the heart (*shubuhat and shahawat)* and realize why knowing about these will helps us cure spiritual diseases. They will also come to appreciate the all-pervasive nature of heedlessness (*ghaflah*) and the central place it occupies amongst the ailments of the heart.
>
> **Objectives**:
> By the end of this lesson the student should be able to:
> 1. **Differentiate** between the categories of *shubuhat* and *shahawat*.
> 2. **Identify** the test al-Ghazali places to assess whether the heart is sick.
> 3. **List** the four ways by which one knows what spiritual ailments one is afflicted with.
> 4. **Describe** what is meant by *ghaflah* and why it is seen by many as being the source of spiritual ills.
> 5. **Mention** what scholars of the heart have stated as cures for heedlessness.

Umar is reported to have said: "There are four types of ocean; passion is the ocean of sins; the nafs is the ocean of desires; death is the ocean of lives; and the grave is the ocean of regret" [Related by Ibn Hajr in Preparing for the Day of Judgment, p20].

1. Shubuhat and shahawat: two sources of spiritual ailments

'[T]rials that afflict the heart are the underlying cause of the ailments of the heart. They are the trials of carnal desires (shahawat) on the one hand and defective understanding and doubts (shubuhat) on the other [...]. The first corrupts one's intention and motive, while the latter corrupts one's cognition and belief." [Ibn al-Qayyim, Ighathatul-Luhfan v1, p11)]

There are two main sources of all the spiritual ailments of the heart - each causes a particular set of spiritual failings. The first of these is the base desires (*shahawat*) that are inbuilt in humans. The breeding ground of these is the alluring nature of the world. The previous module looked at how wrong actions emanating from the limbs affect the spiritual health of the heart. Diseases such as anger, rancor and envy all manifest themselves from this source.

The second is related to spiritual intelligence, where heedlessness of the true aim in life, as well as a defective and tainted understanding (*shubuhat*) of our salvation leads to a host of spiritual diseases such as relying on other than God; displeasure with the divine decree; false hopes or a lack of hope; haste, as well as obliviousness to the blessings received from God.

Most, if not all spiritual diseases of the heart identified by spiritual doctors are in one way or another caused by both *shubuhat* and *shahawat*. If left unchecked, they will jointly lead to the spiritual death of the heart. The Moroccan scholar Ibn 'Ajibah listed three factors that cause a dead heart – namely: love of the world, heedlessness of the remembrance of God and allowing the limbs to freely commit acts of disobedience (itself the definition of heedlessness). *[Iqadh al-Himam, p105]*

2. The purpose of the heart

The way to find out if the heart is spiritually alive is through a simple diagnostic test: look and see if it is performing the task for which it is created. In this section of his renowned work *Ihya*, Imam al-Ghazali provided the necessary test through which one can come to know the spiritual vitality of the heart as well as assess one's progress in curing its ailments. He then pointed out four ways in which we can come to know which particular spiritual diseases we are affected by.

"One should be aware that every organ of the body has been created for a particular purpose. It is only said to be ailing and sick if it is unable to carry out the task for which it was created, such that it is completely incapable of doing so, or only does so after great difficulty. That the hand is ailing is known through it being unable to grasp. That the eye is ailing is known through it being unable to perceive.

And so it is with the illness of the heart, it [is known through] it being unable to fulfill its purpose and carry out the very task for which it was created: that of [attaining] knowledge; spiritual insight (ma'rifah); love of God and His worship; tasting the sweetness of His remembrance by giving it priority over every other desire, indeed making use of every natural human inclination and bodily organ to achieve this purpose: 'And I have not created The Jinn and Men except to worship Me' [51:56]. Every part of the body has a benefit. The benefit of the heart is the attainment of wisdom and spiritual insight (ma'rifah)." [al-Ghazali, Ihya, 3/39]

'You should know that when God intends good for someone He makes apparent for them the shortcomings of their own nafs. One endowed with a penetrating spiritual insight will not be oblivious of their own shortcomings. Once they are aware of the shortcomings it will be possible to treat them. But alas most people are ignorant of their own shortcomings. They see dirt in the eye of their brother yet miss the roots of a tree in their own eye!

3. Four ways of coming to know of the failings of the nafs ('uyub al-nafs)

There are four possible routes for one who wants to find out their own shortcomings:

[3.1] The first is through sitting with one blessed with a deep insight into the 'failings of the nafs' ('uyub al-nafs), one who is acquainted with the hidden illnesses, of which he has complete control of in himself, and then follows his advice and struggles to implement it. […]. This [type of person] is extremely rare to find in this age.

[3.2] To seek out a faithful companion of righteous character endowed with insight, then invest in him the task of critically watching over one's self so that he comes to know one's states and actions. Whatever he finds unbefitting of one's character, actions, inward and outward failings, he should bring them to his attention. This was the path of the wise and great Imams of this community. Umar used to say 'May God show mercy on a person that gives me an insight into my most intimate failings […].

[3.3] Derive knowledge of the failings of one's nafs from what one's enemies say about you since 'the eyes of those looking with contempt magnify one's failings […].

[3.4] That one mix with people. Every time one sees something that is blameworthy one should take oneself to account and ascribe [the trait] to himself. Indeed believers are as mirrors to one another […]. It was said to Jesus [a.s] 'Who taught you manners?' 'No one' he replied. 'I saw the ignorance of the ignorant as a shortcoming and so kept clear of it'. [al-Ghazali, Ihya, 3/96-98]

4. Ghaflah - the source of spiritual ills

"The final reckoning is drawing ever closer for mankind, and yet they turn away out of heedlessness (ghaflah)." [Al-Anbiya:1]

"They know what is apparent of the worldly life, and of the Hereafter they are heedless (ghafilun)." [Ar-Rum:7]

"And the intoxication of death will come in truth: that is what you were trying to avoid. The horn will be blown, that is the Day of which warning had been given. Every soul will come forth, with it an angel to drive it and an angel to bear witness. It will be said: "Indeed you were in ghaflah (heedless) of this, now We have removed from you your covering, and sharp is your sight this Day."" [Qaf:19-22]

4.1 What is ghaflah?

Ghaflah literally means *'overlooking something out of neglect'. It may also be intentional as one says 'I was **heedless** of it' which is used if you left something despite having known about it." [Ibn Faris, Mu'jam, 4/386].*

Imam al-Junayd considered heedlessness to be the source of all diseases of the heart as it leads to one neglecting the divine purpose behind creation and the ultimate end of the human, which is to be judged standing before God. Hence, the Qur'an says *"Indeed you were in ghaflah (heedless) of this, now We have removed from you your covering, and sharp is your sight this Day." [Qaf:19-22]*

All human actions are connected to the presence of an intention behind them, as the intention is a sign of one's awareness. In a hadith related by Abu Hurayrah, it is reported that the Prophet ﷺ said *"Call upon God in a state that you are certain of receiving a response, and know God does not accept a supplication from a heart that is **heedless** and unconcerned." [Ahmed 2/177].*

81

Not only are we warned against having a heedless heart, but the Prophet ﷺ was told to be wary of following after those afflicted by heedlessness:

> "And be patient with those that call upon their Lord during the morning and the evening, desiring nothing but His countenance. Do not allow yourself to overlook them, desiring instead the fleeting adornments of this world. Obey not those whose hearts we have caused to be **heedless** from our remembrance to the point that they follow their own desires while their affair has transgressed all bounds." [al-Kahf: 28].

4.2 Ibn Ata'illah on the effects of heedlessness

One of the most important effects of heedlessness is that a person so afflicted is oblivious to the intimate role that God plays in every moment of their life. Such a person ascribes everything that they will undertake to their own ability and resourcefulness alone, overlooking the fact that every breath they take is known by God and is under His ultimate control. They ascribe any success they achieve as being purely of their own making. When things go wrong, they fall into dismay or even depression, failing to see things in light of the greater wisdom of how things are. In this sense, curing heedlessness leads to a deep contentment with one's fate. In the short aphorism that follows, Ibn 'Ata'illah examines the result of heedlessness. The accompanying commentary explores the relationship this has with one's world view.

> "When one who is heedless wakes in the morning he looks to see what he can do, whereas when the one that is intelligent wakes he looks to see what God will do with him". [al-Hikam, Ibn Ataillah al-Iskandari][48]

> "When one who is heedless wakes in the morning he looks to see what he can do meaning either in his religious affairs or those of the world, to the point that if he is unable to attain what he desires, his state becomes agitated; his disposition becomes changed on account of the feeling of missing out on what he set out to achieve because the means to it have not been attained. All of this is because he relies upon his own actions. Such a person is in constant loss and decrease, even if he may think that he is attaining perfection.

> 'Whereas when the one that is intelligent wakes he looks to see what God will do with him" as a duty which is being sought from him, harnessing his powers, content therein and submitting to this. Such a person does not utilise his time in other than what is required by the command of God.

> It is in relation to this that Ayyub As-Sakhtayani said: 'If what you want does not happen then want what has happened'.

> 'Umar ibn Abdul-Aziz said 'I awake in the morning and I have no pleasure except in the appearance of the divine decree'

> Abu Madyan said 'Be careful that you greet each day putting aside your will and submitting to the decree, in the hope that He looks to you and shows you mercy'.

> Abdul Wahid ibn Abi Zayd said "Contentment is the greatest door to God and the resting place of the worshippers as well as the paradise of this world"" [Zarruq, Sharh al-Hikam, pp213-214].

> "The heedless person is one who is ignorant of God even if he makes profuse mention (dhikr) of Him through his tongue, whereas the intelligent one is he who has knowledge of God, even if the mention (dhikr) done through the tongue be little.

> What is relevant here is the remembrance done through one's heart. The one that is heedless has false and extended hopes and so when he wakes, he looks to see what he can do by himself and so sets in order his affairs and wishes to accomplish things through his own intellect and planning, constantly being self-conscious of his actions, relying totally upon his own power and might. But when destiny obliterates what he has intended and destroys what hopes he had, he becomes angry and ill tempered, loses hope and is affected by covetousness, and so disputes with his Lord and is bad mannered.

---

[48] 'Ghaflatuka fi 'dhikr khayrun min ghaflatuka 'anhu' [Ibn Ata'illah]

What surprise is it that such a person deserves to be distanced from God, and deserves estrangement and rejection in his heart unless he turns back in repentance and remains present, standing at the door [of God] until such a time that the veil is again lifted so that the he becomes amongst the beloved..." [Ibn 'Ajibah, Sharh al-Hikam].

4.3 The cures for heedlessness

'Its cure lies in knowing that God is not heedless of your state. **'And your Lord is not heedless of what you do'** *[Hud:123]. It also comes from knowing that you are to be judged for your thoughts and aspirations. If you find a person who has cured themselves of this ailment, you should closely observe their use of time (raqib awqatahu) and studiously harmonise yourself with their spiritual state (ra'i ahwalahu) so that you too may be freed of the ailment of heedlessness."* [al-Sulami. 'Uyub al-Nafs, p86]

One of the most important steps in purifying the heart is to uphold the dictates of the sacred law by seeking guidance in one's affairs from the Book and the Prophetic norm. Doing this essentially cures heedlessness. Awakening from the spiritual sloth that has affected one's soul is also a requisite of combating heedlessness as *'every spiritual ailment is cured by enacting its opposite'*.

The methods that aid in awakening from heedlessness.

Whoever seeks to do this should:
1- Create a habit of sitting in the company of scholars, those that call to the path of the Lord of the worlds through both their spiritual state and words. This, and lending an attentive ear, with complete presence of heart to the admonitions of the glorious Qur'an and the traditions of the generous Prophet ﷺ.
2- Pondering constantly on death.
3- Having complete surety based on reflection of the death of friends and neighbors.
4- Remembering that one will come before the King and Judge, may He be exalted.
5- Constantly remembering the life to come and pondering over its enduring nature as well as the transitory state of this life.
6- Incessantly opening oneself up (dawam al-tafarugh) to the most Generous and Kind Lord, the Bestower (al-Manan), the Vast (al-'Adhim) with penitence (ruju), seeking of forgiveness (istighfar), weeping and brokenness.
7- Making constant prayer and salutations on His elect Prophet ﷺ, looking out for those who are weak and destitute - with charity, compassion and softness. It is God who guides whom He pleases on the straight path. [al-Habib Ahmed al-Habashi, Tiryaq al-Qulub wal-Asrar, pp34-35]

Lesson Two
Diseases that affect one's understanding and belief [1]

Lesson Two:
Aim: By the end of this lesson students should understand the spiritual diseases of the heart that are related to the *shubuhat* and know their cures.

Objectives:
By the end of this lesson, the students should be able to;
1. **Understand** the nature of *shubuhat* and how particular spiritual ailments relate to them.
2. **Explain** what the ailment *'obliviousness to the blessings received from God'* is and what its cure is.
3. **Explain** what the ailment *'relying on other than God'* is and what its cure is.
4. **Explain** what the ailment *'displeasure with the divine decree'* is and what its cure is.
5. **Mention** what is meant by the statement *"one should be pleased with divine decree but not necessarily with what has been decreed itself."*
6. **Explain** how we can come to know why we have been afflicted by a tribulation?

"Imam Abu Yazid al-Bistami was once asked 'When does a person attain the station of the real men[49]?' He responded "When he is aware of the failings of his own nafs, only then will he have reached that state." [Abu Na'im, Hilyah al-Awliyah, 10/ 37]

1. Diseases that affect one's belief

There are numerous spiritual diseases that man may be afflicted with; rarely is it just one problem that needs attention. Imam Abd al-Rahman al-Sulami in his book entitled *'The Ailments of the Heart and their Cure'* lists sixty-nine spiritual diseases. There are a number of diseases within the heart that stem from a skewed understanding of one's place in the world and a failure to rely upon the true source of one's existence: God. This leads to mislaid priorities as well as a weakness in one's spiritual sight. As outlined in the previous lesson, a deep heedlessness of God (*ghaflah*) precipitates many other symptomatic diseases of the heart related to understanding (*shubuhat*) which are connected to being negligent of the rights owed to God.

The main spiritual ailments of this type are: obliviousness to the blessings received from God; relying on other than God; displeasure with the divine decree; hopelessness; haste; laziness and false extended hopes.

2. Obliviousness to the blessings received from God (kufran al-ni'am)

This is where an individual can no longer see the nature and profuseness of blessings received from God, to the point that gratefulness is no longer shown and thankfulness is not felt. The opposite of this is to express one's gratitude, which in return, leads to an increase.

"This is where the slave of God no longer sees blessings or else is heedless of them such that God is not thanked for having provided them. Blessings are of numerous types, such that they cannot be counted or truly encompassed. As God says: "And if you were to count the blessings of your Lord you would not be able to enumerate them" [Ibrahim:34]. He, may He be praised and exalted, also said "God has struck a similitude: a city that was secure, at rest, its provision coming to it with ease from every place, then it was unthankful for the blessings of God; so God let it taste the garment of hunger and of fear, for the things that they were working." [An-Nahl:112]

2.1 [The cure] - shukr (gratefulness)

"The opposite of this is shukr (gratefulness). It is elevating the One providing blessings for the blessings given, to the point that one never displays aversion to the one providing the blessings. It is also said that shukr is to know the true nature of the blessings. God says "If you show gratitude We will indeed grant you an increase."[Ibrahim:7].

Numan ibn Bashir relates that the Messenger ﷺ said "Whoever does not give thanks for a little will not give thanks for a lot. Whoever does not give thanks to people will not give thanks to God. Speaking about the blessings of God is a type of shukr and leaving it is kufr

---

[49] This term is used by spiritual masters to denote a person that has reached a high station in the path towards God, regardless of their gender.

84

(ungratefulness). The congregation (jama'ah) is [a source of] mercy whereas the small group (firqah) is [a source of] torment." [Ahmed 2:258]

3. Relying on other than God.

"Fear of and desire of other than my Lord
*   contradicts absolute trust in Him.*

The origin of both of them-and I seek refuge in the
*   Mighty from every disease-is lack of certainty"*   [Imam Mawlud]

The desire to please other than God, and the resulting fear associated with such a disease, negates the basic principle of having full and utter reliance on the Creator. Looking to creation as the source of one's strength and wealth shows that there is a lack of certainty in God being the ultimate provider of one's needs.

3.1 [The cure: to reflect on the nature of certainty]

"It is forbidden upon a heart that finds its peace in other than God to smell the sweet scent of certainty." [Sahl ibn Abdillah at-Tustari] [al-Qushayri, Risalah, p289]

This means that one instills in one's heart the certain nature of religious belief. One should see that nothing takes place in the universe except by God's permission; that none has ability to inflict harm or provide ease except by the will of God. Seeing this as a reality that informs our actions will result in our ultimate reliance being on the One upon whom all depend. One should constantly strive in seeking perfect certainty until no doubt remains.

Imam 'Ali[50] said *"If the veil to the realities was to be lifted, I would not increase in certainty."* [Abu Na'im, Hilyah al-Awliyah, 10/ 203]

Dhu' Nun al-Misri said *"Certainty moves one not to have unrealistic hopes, which leads to zuhd (making do with little). Zuhd gives rise to wisdom, which in turn gives rise to one looking into the ultimate course of things (awaqib)."* [al-Qushayri, Risalah, p289]

4. Displeasure with the divine decree

"And amongst people are those that worship God as if it were on the edge. If good befalls him, he is well contended with him, but if a trial afflicts him he reverts to his old ways, losing in both this world and the next. This is the greatest of losses." [Al-Hajj:11]

The secret of the divine decree *(qada & qadar)* is something that God has not disclosed to any creature. To feel displeasure with what has been decreed and what has passed can lead to questioning the wisdom of the One that has decreed it. Through doing so, one is not only expressing one's opposition to the One that decrees, but also barring oneself from the ensuing benefit of patience and certitude that is achieved when one submits to what has been written. The story of Yusuf [a.s] shows the true benefits of submitting to the divine decree and the inevitable rewards that are reserved for such individuals.

"When God makes a wretched man (shaqi')
*   suffer, he flees from Him in ingratitude*
while when He sends suffering to a fortunate man (sa'id)
*   he only moves closer to Him"*
                    [Rumi, Masnavi: 4/2194, Trs. Nicholson]

Indeed the Qur'an constantly reminds the believers of the hidden benefits of what has come to pass, both the bad as well as the good. God says *"It may be that you dislike something though it is good for you and that you may love something, though it is bad for you, and God knows and you do not."* [Al-Baqarah:216].

4.1 [The cure]

The cure to this lies in reflecting over the hidden benefits of what has been written, as well as learning to endure this with patience and certitude and accept that the decree of God is final.

The decreed, both good and bad, is ultimately from God. The response is to act according to what has been decreed. The Prophet ﷺ said in a hadith related by Sohaib ibn Sinan *"How strange is the affair of the*

---

[50] Also related to be a saying of 'Amir ibn 'Abd Qays. *[al-Qushayri, Risalah, p290]*

believer for indeed in all of his matters he is given good, and this is for none except the believer. If he is affected by something which is pleasing, he gives thanks and this is the best course of action. If he is afflicted by an affliction, then he is patient, and this is the best course of action." [Muslim].

4.2 Al-Qarafi on the difference between the decree and what has been decreed

It is important in this context to remember that it is one thing to be content with the divine decree but quite another to use it as an excuse for inaction. One should be pleased with the divine decree, but not necessarily with what has been decreed itself. If what has been decreed is injustice or suffering, it is one's religious duty to address this. Indeed, it is considered to be from the highest acts of worship. The Prophet ﷺ said *"The greatest of jihads is to convey the word of truth in the presence of an unjust ruler"*. The examples of this are many.

> *"Being content with the decree (qada) is an obligation by the consensus of scholars whereas being content with that which is decreed (maqdi) is not. If a doctor prescribes a bitter pill or amputates a diseased hand and the patient says "What a bad diagnosis! Another course of action could have been better and it would have been easier to bear!" This is displeasure with what has been decreed by the doctor. It will harm and offend him such that if the doctor was to hear this he would certainly disapprove and find it difficult to accept.*

> *However if the patient said 'This medicine is bitter that has caused me great hardship and the amputation gave me intense pain' this would be displeasure in what has been decreed (maqdi) - the medicine and amputation - and not the decree itself, which is the actual diagnosis and prescription of the doctor.*

> *This is not taken to be a criticism of the doctor and would not pain him if he caught ear of such a complaint. Rather he would say 'You have realised the reality of the situation."* [Imam al-Qarafi, al-Faruq, V4, p229]

4.3 Understanding hardship

> *Al-Ghazali says "There is no hardship except that it has accompanying it a blessing from God. One should always hold to praising God and thanking Him on account of the blessings that accompany [the hardship]."*

> *Umar said "I have never been afflicted by a difficulty from God except that I found four blessings accompanying it. It is not in my religion; I am not deprived of His pleasure; That it is not worse than it turned out to be and lastly, that I hope for reward on account if it". Imam al-Haramayn said gratitude should be shown in the face of difficulties in this world as they are in reality blessings in disguise. They cause the servant to be met with great benefits, overflowing rewards and [lead to] noble ends. In the face of these [benefits] the hardship accompanying tribulations melt in comparison with these benefits."*

> *It is also related from the 'Arif al-Jilani, may God sanctify his secret: "Taking spiritual pleasure from tribulations is the station of those that know God (Arifin). However this is not given by God to anyone except after them having expended their utmost in seeking His pleasure first."*

> *Tribulations sometimes visit as a result of a transgression; at other times an expiation and cleansing of one's wrong actions; and sometimes they are a means of elevating one's spiritual rank so that one reaches the highest of stations. Each of these has telltale signs.*

> *The sign of the first is that one does not show patience when a trial visits, instead one becomes agitated and complains to people about it. The sign of it being the second type is exercising patience by not expressing one's agitation through complaint. The performance of acts of obedience should also become easier. The sign of the third is that one is pleased and content; obedience by the body as well as the heart also becomes easier. The Prophet ﷺ said "Whoever would like to know their standing in front of God should look to the standing God has in their eyes. Indeed God holds a servant in the same regard as the servant holds God" [al-Hakim]."* [al-Nahlawi, Hadhr wa al-Ibaha, p149].

Lesson Three
Diseases that affect one's understanding and belief [2]

> **Lesson Three:**
> **Aim:** By the end of this lesson students will have continued with their study of the spiritual diseases of the heart that are related to the *shubuhat,* and their cures.
>
> **Objectives**:
> By the end of this lesson, the students should be able to;
> 1. **Explain** what '*hopelessness*' is, what can it lead to and what its cure is.
> 2. **Explain** what '*haste*' is and know what its opposite is.
> 3. **Explain** what '*laziness*' is and what the cure for this is.
> 4. **Explain** what '*false hopes and & ambitions*' are and what the cure for both is.

In this lesson, we will be looking at the remaining spiritual diseases related to a defective understanding of matters (*shubuhat*). These are: *hopelessness, haste, laziness and false hopes and ambitions.*

1. On hopelessness (al-ya's)

"This is constantly remembering what one perceives as having missed out of the Mercy and Grace of God, leading to the heart becoming completely detached, without any inkling of hope. This is disbelief, as is feeling safe from God's plot (makr). This is where one feels safe, certain that one will not be taken to task for transgressions due to a denial of the [divine] quality of Vengeance." [al-Nahlawi, Hadhr wal -Ibaha, p155].

1.1 The cure: al-raja'

Imam al-Nahlawi says that this is cured by reminding ourselves of God's previous favors that He has bestowed upon us.

> 'The opposite of hopelessness is having hope in God's mercy (al-raja') which is the heart being gladdened (ibtihaj al-qalb) on account of the beneficence of God as well as finding comfort in the vastness of His infinite mercy. This is achieved by bringing to mind His previous favors upon us that came to us through no effort or intercessor, the vast reward He has promised us without our having deserved it as well as the fact that His all-encompassing Mercy overrides His Anger.
>
> Say: '[God says:] 'O you servants of Mine who have transgressed against your own selves! Despair not of God's mercy: behold, God forgives all sins – for, verily, He alone is much-forgiving, a dispenser of grace!'"[39:53].
>
> Ibn Masud related that the Messenger of God ﷺ said "God will display such mercy on the Day of Judgment as one cannot even imagine, so much so that Iblis himself will linger in the hope that some reaches him" [Ibn Abi Dunya]" [al-Nahlawi, Hadhr wal -Ibaha, pp 155-156]

2. Haste

> **"Man was created of haste. Assuredly I shall show you My signs; so demand not that I make haste" [Al-Anbiya:37]**
>
> "This is a state which pervades the heart through which an individual either
> [1] Seeks to gain an immediate solution
> [2] Proceeds to do something at the first opportunity whether it is beneficial or not, without reflecting or having looked into the issue enough.
> [3] Seeks to complete something without giving each portion its due. These three elements together encompass the meaning of haste [...].

2.1 Effects of haste

The **first** type leads to apathy (futur), a break from performing good acts, and not achieving one's objective [...] 'since one that is over-exuberant will neither cover any distance, nor be left with a mount'[51].

The **second** type leads to a loss of taqwa and scrupulousness since one starts to do an act which is harmful without any reflection [...].

The **third** type leads to a decrease or total invalidity of the action being done due to a lack of the requisite etiquette, sunnah or, worse still, wajib or fard elements. A person who makes haste while in prayer may miss the three tasbih in bowing and prostration or else change the dhikr and mix them from their proper place [...].

2.2 The cure: 'anah (deliberation)

"The direct opposite of this is 'anah (deliberation).

The opposite of the first - to gain an immediate solution - is to wait in the best way (husn al-intidhar).

The opposite of the second - to do something whether it is beneficial or not at the first opportunity - is to take one's time and become firm in one's resolve until the right path becomes clear.

The opposite of the third - seeking to complete something without giving each portion its due - is giving something due deliberation (al-'anah) so that one gives everything due consideration. The Messenger 🌸 said "Considered silence (al-samt al-hassan), giving things due consideration and prudence (iqtisad) are a twenty-fourth portion of Prophecy."[52]

[...] However, one should not take deliberation to be equivalent to delaying things or putting things off (taswif), since it is related that the Prophet 🌸 said 'Deliberation is good in all things except actions relating to the Hereafter.' [Abu Dawud]. It is also related that Hatim al-'Assam said "Haste is from the shaytan except in five things, since it is from the Prophetic sunnah: feeding guests; preparing a dead body for burial; marrying off the virgin; settling one's debts; and repenting from wrong actions." [al-Nahlawi, Hadhr wal -Ibaha, Pp141- 143]."

2.3 On the merits of deliberation

It is related that when the tribe of Abd al-Qays came as a delegation from Bahrain to meet the Prophet 🌸 in Madinah, they were so eager to meet him that, even after the toil of the extended journey through the desert, and having barely placed their bags on the ground, they all ran to greet the Prophet 🌸. The Messenger greeted them and welcomed them warmly to the city. All this time, one of the party, Al-Ashajj 🌸, was busying himself in preparation to meet the Prophet 🌸, and having bathed and put on his best attire and perfume, he went to the Prophet 🌸 in all calmness. *"When he arrived to the Prophet 🌸, he took hold of the blessed hand of the Prophet 🌸 and kissed it. The Prophet 🌸 said to him "You have two qualities beloved to God and His Messenger: forbearance (hilm) and deliberation ('anah)." He said 'Messenger of God, are they qualities that I have cultivated by myself or ones God has created inherently within me?' He said 'Rather God has created them inherently within you'. He then exclaimed 'Praise be to God who has inherently created within me two qualities beloved to God and His Messenger!'"* [Abu Dawud]

3. Laziness.

'From the ailments that afflict the heart is laziness (kasl), the breeding ground of which is satiation and excessive eating. When the nafs is satiated it gains strength, and it then takes whatever license it can, thereby overpowering the heart to attain its goal.

3.1 The cure for laziness

---

[51] Part of a Prophetic tradition narrated in Musnad Ahmed, v3, pg197

[52] *al-Tirmidhi on the authority of Abdullah ibn Sarjas.*

88

"The cure for this is hunger, as once it is afflicted with hunger the portion of the nafs diminishes and weakens. The heart thereby takes control. When it does so, it moves it towards obedience thereby removing laziness. This is why the Prophet ﷺ said "The son of Adam has never filled a vessel worse than the stomach. Sufficient for a son of Adam are some morsels to keep his back straight. But if he must, then let one-third be for his food, one-third for his drink and one-third for breathing." [Ahmad][Abd al-Rahman al-Sulami, 'Uyub al-Nafs, p44]

4. False hopes ('amani)

*"Its quick acting poison is extended false hope which is
assuring yourself that death is a long way off.*

*This generates hard heartedness and indolence regarding
obligations which leads to inroads to the prohibited".   [Imam Mawlud]*

"The consequences of this are:
[1] Laziness in performing good actions, or delaying them.
[2] Leaving of performing repentance or else the complete abandoning of it.
[3] Hardness of heart due to a neglect of remembering death and what occurs after it.
[4] Covetousness regarding acquiring goods of this world in large numbers due to a fear of old age, illness and the like."

4.1 The cure - Remembering one's mortality.

The strongest cure for this is a constant reflection over one's mortality, as well as lending one's ear to what has been related regarding this. One should know that false hopes, if they be on account of partaking in pleasures that are forbidden, then it is conclusively forbidden otherwise it is not necessarily so, but is strongly condemned on account of the aforementioned illnesses' [al-Nahlawi, Hadhr wal -Ibaha, pp 106- 107].

5. Postface: Al Muhasibi on the effects of certainty and knowledge

"Know that when a person has truly obtained knowledge and his certainty has been established:
-He knows that nothing can save him from His Lord except truthfulness, hence he strives for that. He observes the manners of its people so that he can realise it in his life before death arrives. This is because he wants to prepare for the eternal abode which follows death. He sells his soul and his wealth for Allah when he hears Him say: "Indeed, God has purchased from the believers their lives and their properties in exchange for which they will have Paradise." [9:111]

Hence he learned after being in ignorance, became free of need after being in poverty, became affable after being secluded, came closer after being far, got respite after being in struggle. His affair is harmonised and his resolve is gathered.

His motto is having trust [in God], and his state is the state of Muraqabah. Don't you see the statement of the Messenger of God ﷺ: "Worship God as though you can see Him, and if you can't see Him then indeed He is seeing you."

The ignorant thinks that he is an inarticulate man having nothing to say, rather it is his wisdom that has kept him quiet. The fool thinks he is being talkative, rather his sincerity for God has made him speak. He is thought to be rich when it is abstinence that has enriched him. He is thought to be poor, rather it is the humility of his that makes him so.

He does not interfere with matters that do not concern him. He does not bear beyond what suffices him. Neither does he take of what he is not in need of, nor does he let go what he has been entrusted to look after. People are in comfort being around him, yet he is always pressured within himself. He put to death his cravings through his piety, put an end to his greed through his taqwa and annihilated his desires through the light of his knowledge.

Therefore, be exactly like this man. Befriend such people. Follow their footsteps. Refine yourself with their manners. Truly they are the reliable treasures." [Abu Abdillah Al Muhasibi, Risalatul Mustarshidin" pp105-10]

Lesson Four
Replacing God with the world

> **Lesson Four:**
> **Aim:** By the end of this lesson students will come to understand the nature of the world and how being negatively connected to it gives rise to a number of spiritual ailments.
>
> **Objectives:**
> By the end of this lesson students should be able to:
> 1. **Discuss** the allure of the world and its role in giving rise to spiritual diseases.
> 2. **Explain** the hadith *"Do not curse the world, for how good it is! Being the riding-beast of the believer!"*
> 3. **Explain** what *'love of the world'* is and the two cures mentioned in this regard.
> 4. **Differentiate** between the *'zuhd'* and *'qanah'*.
> 5. **Explain** what *'miserliness'* is and the cure mentioned for this.

Echoes from the world

> *"This world is like a steep valley which echoes. Whatever you say, whatever you do, whatever you think or feel, good or bad, returns back to you louder as an echo. Of course you wish that the echo be melodious and sweet. But alas no! If the mountain could speak, it would say: "I have no will of my own, I am but your shadow, your echo. Whatever you are, I show! This world is but the arable field of the hereafter. Whatever you plant here will be harvested in the Hereafter." [Al-Birgavi, pp337-338]*

1. The reality of the world

Heedlessness of the purpose in life will inevitably lead to an attachment to the world. This in turn produces symptomatic spiritual ailments which include an intense love of the temporal world (*hubb ad-dunyah*) to the point that one forgets about preparing for the life to come, develops an unhealthy preoccupation (*hirs*) with acquiring one's livelihood and exhibits the extremes of miserliness (*bukhl*) and spend-thriftiness (*israf*).

The general cure for all of these is to understand the true nature of the world and the way that the believer is advised to deal with its inevitable distractions.

> *"The parable of the life of this world is but that of rain which We send down from the sky, and which is absorbed by the plants of the earth whereof men and animals draw nourishment, until – when the earth has assumed its artful adornment and has been embellished, and they who dwell on it believe that they have gained mastery over it – there comes down upon it Our judgment, by night or by day, and We cause it to become [like] a field mown down, as if there had been no yesterday. Thus clearly do We spell out these messages unto people who think!" [Yunus:24]*

The word for the world in Arabic is *dunya*, which literally means *that which is lowly*. Compared with the unending reality that is the next world, the world is described as being similar to what remains upon one's finger after having placed it within the ocean. Because of this, all Prophets instructed their followers to be wary of becoming attached to the allure of its distractions. The Prophet Jesus ﷺ said *"The world is a bridge; so pass over it to the next world, but do not try to build on it."*

"Ibn 'Abbas reported 'I heard the Prophet ﷺ *as saying, "If the son of Adam had two valleys of gold, he would wish for a third, for nothing can fill the belly of Adam's son except for dust, and God forgives him who repents to Him." [Bukhari]*

The Islamic tradition has a balanced view of the world, condemning it when it diverts one from God, and praising it when it is used for the common good. The Prophet ﷺ said *"The world is cursed and all that is within it, except the remembrance of God and that which aids it, or one who teaches and the one that learns" [Ibn Majah, 4112].* On the other hand, it is reported that the Prophet ﷺ said *"Do not curse the world, for how good it is! Being the riding-beast of the believer!" [al-Daylami, Musnad).* Hence, if what one has of the world is used for the betterment of one's Hereafter and as a vehicle for good, it is viewed as the source of virtue.

Not only does love of the world lead to many of the spiritual ailments of the heart, it is the source of collective weakness.

> Al-Thawban related that the Messenger ﷺ said *'Nations will call each other, as people make invitations to a meal, to make a concerted attack on you." Someone asked: "Will this happen because there are only a few of us?" God's Messenger answered: "No, your numbers will be vast, but you will be as powerless as the flotsam and jetsam carried in a flood. God will remove your enemies' fear of you. You will have 'wahn' planted in your hearts. They asked "and what is 'wahn', Messenger of God?" He replied "Fear of death and a love of the world." [Ibn Hanbal, 5/278]*

The diseases related to *replacing God with the world*

2. Love of the world

> *"Know that the life of this world is but a play and a passing delight, and a beautiful show, and [the cause of] your boastful vying with one another, and [of your] greed for more and more riches and children. [Its parable is that of [life-giving] rain: the herbage which it causes to grow delights the tillers of the soil; but then it withers, and thou canst see it turn yellow; and in the end it crumbles into dust. But [the abiding truth of man's condition will become fully apparent] in the life to come: [either] suffering severe, or God's forgiveness and His goodly acceptance: for the life of this world is nothing but an enjoyment of self-delusion." [Hadid: 20].*

> *Aishah reported the Prophet ﷺ as saying "The world is an abode for he who has no abode and those that come together to attain it are [like] those who possess no intellect" [Ahmed]. He ﷺ also said "Whoever has the Hereafter as their constant concern, God will place self-sufficiency in his heart and will gather its strength for him and the world will come to him despite itself [raghima]. Whosoever has the world as his constant concern, God will place poverty in front of his very eyes and will scatter his strength and he will [still only] attain of the world what is written for him." [At-Tirmidhi].*

> *One can find many [Qur'anic] verses as well as Prophetic traditions in condemnation of the world.*

> *The reason for this is that it is an obstacle to the worship of God and leads to wrong actions and what is forbidden except for one granted felicity by God. Hasan al-Basri said "Love of the world is the source of every wrong action." [al-Nahlawi, pp137-138].*

2.1 Cures for love of the world

2.1.1 Doing without in the world (zuhd)

A person wrote to Sufyan al-Thawri seeking advice and he replied *"Work for the world according to the time you spend therein, and strive for the next world according to your continual inhabitance of it. Peace!"* [Ibn Khalikan, Wafayat al-'Ayan 2/ 387]

> *"The opposite of this [i.e. love of the world] is doing without (zuhd) where one does not find their heart inclining to seek it out or acquire it. Therefore zuhd can be defined as 'the heart being empty of the world and not necessarily that the hand be empty of it'.*
> *There are three types of wealth on the earth: minerals, vegetation and livestock. These have all been brought together in the words of God "Decked out for mankind is the love of lusts - women, children, heaped-up stocks of gold and silver, horses of distinction, cattle and tillage. That is the enjoyment of the present life..." ['Aali-Imran:14]*

> *These items have two types of relationships with an individual;*
> *Firstly, a connection with the heart, which is love (hubb) of these things. Subsumed within this are all of the [negative] qualities of the heart related to the world such as arrogance, rancour, envy, ostentation, showing off and the like.*

> *Secondly, a relationship with one's body which consists of preoccupying oneself in suitably utilising these things in order for them to be fit for the job and [also to] be useful for others as well. This encompasses all of the professions and occupations which mankind is busy in performing.*

Mankind has only come to forget themselves, their ultimate purpose and their journey through the world on account of these two relationships, meaning the relationships with the heart in terms of love and the relationships with the body in terms of pre-occupation (shughl)." [al-Nahlawi, pp138-9]

2.1.1.1 The predicament relating to *zuhd*

"Ahmed al-Zarruq said "Abu Abbas al-Hadrami said to me 'The predicament is not [that of] who knows how to remove oneself from the world, leaving it [altogether] but rather [that of] who knows the manner in which to take hold of it and control it". I [al-Zarruq] say "This is because it is like a snake, as it is not a great feat that you kill it, but rather what is impressive is to take hold of the snake while it is alive.'

According to the hadith "Zuhd is not that you prohibit [yourself from] the halal or give away wealth, rather zuhd is that you have more confidence in what is in the hand of God than you have with what is in your own hand." [at-Tirmidhi 2340][az-Zaruq, Qawaid, p226]

Cures for love of the world

2.1.2 *Contentment (qanah')*

"This is to make do with little of the world and not seek an increase. This cannot reach fruition save through a number of factors:

(1) *Economy in one's lifestyle as well as moderation in expenditure. This is the route of contentment since whoever has many outgoings will inevitably have to spend widely, in which case contentment will not suitably take hold. The Prophet ﷺ said "He who practices economy will never be poor";*

(2) *To have certainty that the sustenance that has been assigned for him will no doubt come his way, as it would come even if he were to become extremely covetous;*

(3) *To know the rank of contentment in terms of the honour of being without need [istighnah] and [to know] what covetousness (hirs) and mudahanah (being hypocritical in one's dealings with others for some benefit) contains in terms of abasement;*

(4) *That one looks to the qualities of the Prophets and listens to their words, such that one will be able to make do with having patience with little and contentment with a small amount;*

(5) *To look at those who are less well off in the world and not to those that are above oneself.*

It is through these things that one can attain the quality of contentment. The source of all this is patience. The Prophet ﷺ said "Whoever wakes in the morning with [the blessing of] safety for his dependents and good health, possessing sufficient food for the day: It is as if the world has been brought together for him in all of its facets". The Prophet ﷺ said "The Holy spirit brought inspiration into my soul that no soul dies until it completes in attaining its sustenance, so fear God and be graceful in seeking." [al-Nahlawi, p140].

3. Miserliness (*bukhl*)

"Satan threatens you with the prospect of poverty and bids you to be niggardly, whereas God promises you His forgiveness and bounty; and God is infinite, all-knowing." [Al-Baqarah:268]

"It is a [negative] quality of the heart which calls one to keep hold of wealth at times when it is obligatory that it be spent, either in accordance [with the dictates of] the sacred law or chivalry (maruw'ah). The worst type of miserliness is to withhold spending on oneself in such a way as not to allow oneself to eat or consume from one's own wealth, or clothe or treat oneself, or treat oneself with medicine. This is also called shuh (covetousness).

God says "For such as from their own covetousness (shuh) are saved – it is they, they that shall attain to felicity!" [Hashr:9]

God says "Do not consider those that are miserly with what God has given them from his bounty that this is better for them, but rather it is worse for them. What they were miserly with will be made into a necklace for them on the day of judgement." ['Aali-Imran: 180].

Abu Bakr said "Paradise will not be entered by a trickster, a miser and one who makes constant mention of his favours to them" [At-Tirmidhi].

Miserliness has been condemned in verses of the Qur'an and many hadith and it is, when it goes against the dictates of law, forbidden - and when it goes against the dictates of virtuousness, makruh. Whoever fulfills the obligation of the law and the obligations of virtuousness in a way that befits him is free from miserliness." [al-Nahlawi, p131]

3.1 The cure for miserliness

3.1.1 Reflecting over the nature of miserliness

"To reflect profusely upon the related narrations regarding the unseemliness of miserliness, the praise of generosity as well as what God has promised upon the miser of intense torment.

A good, beneficial medicine for this is reflecting over the state of people that are miserly - the fact that people are naturally repulsed by them, viewing them as extremely ugly. There is no miser except that other people are repulsed by him. Even misers find other misers difficult to be with..." [al-Nahlawi, p132]

3.1.2 Generosity

"The opposite of miserliness is generosity and virtue - qualities in an individual that move them to expend more wealth than they are required to, for no other reason than to acquire the reward or meritoriousness of cleansing the soul from the lowliness of miserliness. However, one should be careful not to fall into spend-thriftiness. The highest level of generosity is called 'Ithar' which is to expend one's wealth on others while being personally in need of it.

God says: "They prefer them before themselves, even though poverty may afflict them. For such as from their own covetousness (shuh) are saved – it is they, they that shall attain to a happy state!" [Hashr: 9]

Aishah related that the Prophet ﷺ said "A friend of God (wali) is not predisposed to any quality as much as generosity and good character. [Abu Shaykh]" [al-Nahlawi, ibd, p132]

4. Postface - Shaykh Ahmed az-Zarruq on organisation

"Organise your time in a manner appropriate to the time's specific needs, using gentleness and toleration, and be wary of either harshness or laxity. This is because too much laxity concerning permissible matters pulls the heart backwards in its journey until even a man of resolve ends up looking like a foolish boy. Work for this world as if you will live forever, but work for the next life as if you will die tomorrow. Thus do not neglect the external [aspects] of your worldly needs. In the meantime, do not be heedless of your destiny and final resting place....

Organise your devotional practices and you will find your time is extended due to the baraka (blessings) in it. Never be fanatical about anything, whether in regards to the truth or falsehood; this way your heart will remain in a state of soundness towards others. Never claim anything you are entitled to, let alone what you are not entitled to. This way you will be safe from tricks and treachery. This is because anyone who claims some rank above his own will fall in humiliation, while those who claim a rank they warrant will have it stripped from them. But those who claim a station less than their true rank will be elevated to higher levels than they actually deserve." [Ahmed az-Zarruq, quoted from Yusuf, Purification of the Heart, p200]

Lesson Five
The emergence of the ego and self-consciousness 1

> **Lesson Five:**
> **Aim:** By the end of this lesson students should have understood those spiritual diseases that are connected with the ego or '*nafs*' such as vanity and arrogance - and how they come about.
>
> **Objectives**:
> By the end of this lesson the students should be able to;
> 1. **Discuss** the significance of the ego in giving rise to certain diseases of the heart.
> 2. **Explain** what sanctimony (*raya'*) is and what the cure for it is.
> 3. **Explain** what '*love of worldly leadership*' is and what the three underlying reasons for it are.
> 4. **Explain** what vanity is and know the relationship it has with the other diseases in this section, explaining how this understanding helps in administering a cure for it.
> 5. **Explain** what arrogance (*kibr*) is and how it relates to vanity.
> 6. **Mention** what the difference between *kibr* and *takabur* is.
> 7. **Discuss** the cure for arrogance.

1. The ego and self-consciousness

> "Sufyan al-Thawri said "Every act of disobedience committed due to passion, its forgiveness is hoped for. Every act of disobedience committed due to arrogance, its forgiveness is not hoped for the root of Satan's disobedience was arrogance, whereas the root of Adam's lapse was passion." [Ibn Hajr, Preparing for the Day of Judgment, p2]

Central to the ailments of the heart are those that are related to the nature of our self-consciousness. This group of spiritual diseases is the most dangerous and destructive of all ailments because of its effects on others.

The first wrong action in the heavens was that of *Iblis*, who, out arrogance, stated that he was better than the first human that God created. The first wrong action on earth was that of envy, where one of the sons of Adam [a.s] killed his brother because God accepted his brother's sacrifice rather than his own. The source of this envy was another of the major spiritual ailments – namely, vanity ('*ujb*), which is itself the product of heedlessness (*ghaflah*) and arrogance (*kibr*). The associated desire for worldly power and influence, together with the fear of being criticised whilst attempting to arrive at such power, are all the result of the self (*nafs*) consolidating and strengthening its attachment to the *dunya*.

As Imam al-Nahlawi states *"[Worldly goods have] a connection with the heart, which is love (hubb) of these things. Hidden within this are all the qualities of the heart related to the world such as arrogance, rancour, envy, ostentation, showing off and the like."* [al-Nahlawi, pp 138-9].

2. Love of fame *(hubb al-Jah)*

> "The Prophet ﷺ said "Two hungry wolves set loose on a flock of sheep are not more destructive [to one's soul] than covetousness and publicity [are] upon his religion" [at-Tirmidhi].
>
> The underlying reasons for this are three;
> -Firstly, to attain what is forbidden of the desires and wishes of the self, through fame. This is haram.
> -Secondly, to use it in order to obtain one's right or attain a praiseworthy goal or something that is permissible or to remove injustice [...]. If this is free of reprehensible matters such as ostentation [...] it is permitted, rather it is recommended. Otherwise it is not allowed since it is done for a reason that is, at its source, blameworthy. Good intent will have no effect in this case [...].
> -Thirdly, to seek it for its own sake, considering it to be a type of perfection, such as being attached to wealth simply in order to enjoy it. This, if it is free from that which is blameworthy, will not be forbidden. However, it is considered to be frowned upon on account of the person having a very restricted concern.

2.1 The cure

The cure for this is to know that it is not complete perfection, because it can disappear anytime and is tainted. The strongest path to alleviating the desire for fame is to seclude oneself from people by keeping to a state of obscurity." [Al-Nahlawi, p95].

3. On sanctimony (al-ri'ya')

"The origin of sanctimony is seeking to gain a place in the hearts of man through making a show of one's good actions." [al-Ghazzali, v5: p336]

"Sanctimony is to seek worldly gain through acts meant for the Hereafter. The opposite of this is ikhlas, which is to free acts of worship done to gain closeness to God from any worldly utility. God says "and they were not ordered except to worship God making the faith purely for him." [al-Bayyinah:5]. [al-Nahlawi, p104]

3.1 The cure - knowing its causes and opposite

"The opposite of this is ikhlas (sincerity), which is to free acts of worship done to gain closeness to God from any worldly utility or making it known. It gives birth to ihsan, which is that 'you worship God as if you see Him, and if you do not, know that He sees you' [...]

'The cure for sanctimony lies in knowing its causes and preliminaries as well as knowing how its opposite (sincerity) is nurtured and what benefits it holds. [...]

The causes of sanctimony are love of fame and the desire to occupy a place in peoples' hearts [...]

The benefits sincerity hold are: the achievement of God's pleasure, one's actions being accepted, as well as success and increase in the Hereafter.

Once this is understood, the cure can be seen to lie in two things: cutting the branches and ripping out its roots by removing what causes it on the one hand, as well as by striving to attaining its opposite (sincerity)." [al-Birgivi, al-Tariqah al-Muhammadiyyah, pp46-66].

4. Vanity (al-'ujb)

"This is defined as thinking highly of a blessing received and relying upon it, while at the same time forgetting to ascribe it to the real source of the blessing, who is God. Being preoccupied with the blessing rather than remembering the one giving the blessing is vanity and blameworthy [...].
The origin of vanity in reality is pure ignorance (jahl), heedlessness (ghaflah) and forgetfulness (nisyan).

4.1 Vanity in knowledge

The worst type of vanity is that related to holding a false opinion which one is pleased with and holds dear, leading to one not listening or paying heed to the advice of others, viewing them as ignorant. God says "Is he for whom his evil actions have been made to appear to him as an adornment, to the point that they see it to be good..." [Fatir:8].

All heretical groups and those that have gone astray have only held closely to their views due to their being pleased with them.
The cure for this vanity [of holding a false opinion] is more difficult and elusive [than mere vanity] since the person with this quality considers it to be knowledge, not ignorance, a blessing and not a test, something healthy and not a sickness. Therefore they do not seek out a cure and refuse to give ear to the spiritual physicians who are well versed with the ailments of the heart and who administer its cures - namely the scholars of the Ahl-Sunnah wal-Jamah, may God give victory to their positions until the Day of Judgement.

4.2 Cure

The general cure is knowledge that everything is through the creation of God and His Will and that each blessing, whether it be intelligence, knowledge, action, reputation, wealth or something else, is from God alone [...]

The strongest cure for [vanity] is knowledge of its [associated] ailments, which are many. Suffice it to say that it is the source of arrogance, forgetfulness of wrong actions, forgetfulness of the blessings of God as well as a feeling of safety from the plan (makr) of God and His punishment.

It is also, [to believe] that God owes one a favor and a right on account of one's actions, which are in fact a blessing from amongst His blessings and a gift from His gifts. This calls a person to speak highly of themselves, thereby leaving them bereft of benefiting and taking counsel from others. Anas said that the Prophet ﷺ said "There are three deadly sins; extreme greed, a desire upon which one acts, and a person being vain about themselves. [al-Bayhaqi]" [Al-Nahlawi pp114-5].

5. Arrogance (kibr)

"Arrogance is defined as seeking pleasure and comfort in one's own nafs, while at the same time imposing this state on a person shown the arrogance. That there be one that arrogance is shown to is a necessary component of the definition as opposed to the case with vanity ('ujb) as it does not require that there be one to whom one's vanity is displayed.

Arrogance is condemned, since, as well as being an immensely negative quality for a servant to have - being the path of Iblis the cursed - is also the most despicable of blameworthy characteristics.
The person possessing this quality attempts to vie with God in His Haughtiness and Greatness. This, if it is manifested outwardly, is called **takabur** *and if hidden internally, is called* **kibr.**
Ibn Masud said that the Prophet ﷺ said "No one who has an atom's weight of arrogance in his heart will enter paradise". A person said "One loves that they have beautiful clothing and beautiful sandals." He said "God is beautiful and loves beauty." [Muslim].

5.1 The cure

5.1.1 Removing its cause

The cause of arrogance *in reality is* **ignorance** *(jahl) and its cure is through the removal of its cause [...]. Know that arrogance may be hidden from the person possessing this quality to the point that he may think that he is free of it. Therefore, it is necessary to explain the characteristics of those that are arrogant, so that each [person] takes a reflective look at themselves, so that the impure be differentiated from the pure."*

[Section on characteristics of the arrogant]
Amongst these are:
- *A desire that people stand for him or in front of him as a mark of respect.*
- *that he never walk except with somebody else follow behind*
- *that he never visit anybody, out of arrogance*
- *that he detest that anyone sit next to him in close proximity*
- *that he avoid sitting with those that are ill or disabled out of a feeling of arrogance or haughtiness, similarly avoiding the company of the poor and destitute*
- *that he detest the invitation of the poor, but not of the rich and well-heeled in society*
- *that he detest wearing clothes that are not of a certain standard*
- *that he not participate himself in the chores of his house*
- *that he not carry his own goods to his house*
- *that he detest fulfilling the needs of his relatives and friends, especially buying of menial things for them.*
- *that he be bothered by his peers walking in front of him or sitting before him*
- *refusal to accept the truth when debating with peers, refusing to accept mistakes, refusing to show gratitude for this as well as not reflecting over someone else's advice, as a means of belittling the other person or out of enmity or arrogance.*

All of these characteristics, if they occur in a large congregation, are considered to be part of ostentation (al-riya') and showing-off in, desiring to appear to people as being perfect, covering over shortcomings, feigning possession of qualities that one does not possess.

If they do exist and this occurs in private then it is described as arrogance (kibr).

96

5.1.2 Humility

The opposite of this is humility (tawadu'), which is where one views oneself as below other people. This is a great quality in an individual. Making this known, whereby one makes oneself appear below one's actual rank is considered praiseworthy humility. However, if done more than that it is considered to be disingenuous to the point of being blameworthy, except when seeking knowledge. If it is excessive then it is nothing but a self centred desire, which is haram." [Al-Nahlawi, pp108-110].

6. Postface: Imam 'Ali on the sunnah

Ali said:"He who does not possess the 'sunnah of God', the sunnah of His Messenger ﷺ and the sunnah of his chosen ones, in fact has nothing." He was asked "What is the sunnah of God?" He replied "Safeguarding people's secrets". When asked concerning the sunnah of His Messenger ﷺ, he replied "Being gentle with people". Finally, he was asked of the sunnah of His chosen ones: he said "Bearing people's harm."' [Ibn Hajr, Preparing for the Day of Judgment, p11].

Lesson Six
The emergence of the ego and self-consciousness 2

> **Lesson Six**
>
> **Aim**: By the end of this lesson, the students should have completed their understanding of those spiritual diseases that are connected with the Ego or '*Nafs*'. They will also have looked at what are described as the *"The Comprehensive treatments of the Heart'*
>
> **Objectives**:
> By the end of this lesson students should be able to:
> 1. **Discuss** what al-Ghazzali mentioned regarding the origin of anger and how he relates this to rancor and envy.
> 2. **Detail** the four methods of curing anger.
> 3. **Mention** what is meant by rancor and how it differs from anger.
> 4. **Explain** what envy (*hasd*) is and how is it cured?
> 5. **Discuss** what was said regarding the comprehensive treatments of the heart.
> 6. **Discuss** what it means to '*take refuge in God (al-firar ila Allah)*' in the light of what scholars of the heart have said.

"Bury your existence in the earth of obscurity. Since that which sprouts before it is buried-its produce will never come to fruition" [Ibn Ata'illah al-Iskandari]

In the literature on the diseases of the heart, there are three ailments that are mentioned together due to their close connection with one another. They are all related to the aggressive expansion of the ego over other people. They are anger, rancor and envy. The cures for each of these are practical, proactive and closely linked, and they [the diseases] can also be treated by what is known as the comprehensive cure for all spiritual diseases: taking refuge in God (*al-firar ila Allah*).

1. Anger

Few spiritual diseases have such clear ramifications in the outside world as the emotion of anger. The desire for fame, personal vanity and arrogance all provide a fertile breeding ground for rage and violence to take hold. Whether it be between individuals or between civilisations, few could argue that venting anger in a manner that is not informed by the teachings of the Prophets leads to transgression and ultimately, injustice.

This is why the treatment of this ailment was considered to be so important by the Prophet ﷺ. Upon being asked by a man for advice, he replied *"Do not become angry."* Upon being pressed again and again to offer other advice the Prophet ﷺ reiterated *"Do not become angry"*.

Al-Ghazali on anger

> *"Anger is a spark of fire extracted from the blazing fire of God which envelopes the hearts of men. It has taken up residence in the folds of the heart in the same way that a piece of coal takes up residence beneath sooty ash. It is extracted through arrogance which is buried in the hearts of every arrogant, argumentative one in the same way that fire extracts steel from stone.*
> *It has been unveiled through the light of certainty, for those that have inner perception, that man has a vein connecting him to the accursed Shaytan. The essence of Shaytan has been strengthened within whoever is lured by the fire of anger. He said "You created me from fire and you created him from clay".*
> *The nature of soil is that it is still and tranquil. The nature of fire is that it burns and scolds, constantly moving and fluctuating.*
> *The results of anger are rancour (hiqd) and envy (hasad) and through these is the destruction of he who is destroyed and the downfall of he who falls down.*
> *What will ultimately benefit them is a lump of flesh, which, if it is healthy, the whole body gains its health." [Al-Ghazali, Ihya, v3, p238].*

1.1 The cures for anger

> *"Anger is an illness that has far reaching negative ramifications and is difficult to cure and treat. There is no getting away from exerting oneself in the utmost, rolling one's sleeves up and*

battling against it. It is treated by one of four things; (1) Knowledge (2) Action (3) Removing its underlying cause (4) Acquiring its opposite, which is forbearance (hilm).

1.1.1 Knowledge

One treatment is knowing its shortcomings and the benefit of suppressing one's rage. As for its shortcomings they are of four types;

1.1.1.1 *Ravaging the source of all good actions - faith itself. Much of what is produced by extreme anger - in terms of words or actions - necessitates disbelief;*

1.1.1.2 *The fear one should have of God repaying this in a similar manner, for indeed God's ability over you is far greater than that which you have over this individual. If you were to give vent to your anger, you have no surety that God will not proceed in taking you to task with His;*

1.1.1.3 *Creating enemies: your enemy rolling up his sleeves to confront you, striving to undermine your intent and afflicting you with tribulations, thereby destroying your life and livelihood to the point that you cannot busy yourselves with either knowledge or action;*

1.1.1.4 *The ugliness of your face when angry, remembering how it resembles a rabid dog and a predatory animal ...].*

1.1.2 Action

This is made up of four things;

1.1.2.1 *Performing ablution.[53]*

1.1.2.2 *Sitting. If this works then so be it, otherwise one should lie down.[54]*

1.1.2.3 *To seek refuge in God from the accursed Shaytan.[55]*

1.1.2.4 *Reciting the supplication that is related in this regard: "O God forgive me for my transgression and remove the rancor of my heart and save me from the Shaytan." [Ibn As-Sunni].*

1.1.3 Removing its underlying cause

This is the pro-active treatment. Striving to remove the desire for fame, arrogance and vanity - since a person having these three qualities becomes angry due to the smallest thing that he imagines as being seen as a slight therein.

1.1.4 Acquiring forbearance

This is greater than suppressing one's rage, and the path to acquiring it is to actively demonstrate forbearance over a period of time (tahallum), which is to force one's nafs to constantly and meticulously suppress anger time and again so that it becomes a natural trait and characteristic.

It is related that one of the early Muslims said "I acquired the quality of forbearance by living with a bad tempered, foul mouthed man for a long period of time. I used to be patient enduring the harm he caused me, suppressing my anger to the point that this quality became part of my nature". This is also the way that one may acquire all the cardinal virtues such as humility, generosity and courage." [Al-Nahlawi, p121-123].

2. On rancor (hiqd)

"Rancor (hiqd) is holding internal enmity and hostility for another. It manifests [itself] as making oneself see another as burdensome, annoying, having hatred for them, wishing that harm and evil befall them each time that they come to mind or are seen.

---

[53] *The Prophet* 📛 *said "Anger is from the Shaytan and indeed the Shaytan is created from fire and the only thing that puts out fire is water, and so if one of you becomes angry let them perform wudu" [Abu Dawud]*

[54] *Abu Dharr relates that the Prophet* 📛 *said to him that "If one of you becomes angry while standing then let them be seated and if this causes the anger to subside then so be it, otherwise they should lie down" [Abu Dawud]*

[55] *Sulayman ibn Sard related "Two men exchanged abuse in the presence of the Prophet* 📛 *whilst we were there. While one of them was abusing the other in anger, his face red with rage, the Prophet* 📛 *said "I will teach you some words which, if he was to repeat them, what he finds in himself would go away. If he says "I seek in refuge in God from the accursed devil" what he finds in himself will leave him'"[Bukhari and Muslim]*

The legal ruling related to it is that if the rancor (hiqd) is not due to having been wronged, such as if it was on account of a right [being defended] or to do justice, such as enjoining what is good and forbidding what is bad, in such a case the rancour (hiqd) is prohibited (haram).

If, however, it comes as a result of being wronged, rancor (hiqd) is not prohibited. If the person is unable to gain redress, they can either leave aside demanding redress until the Day of Resurrection or else show clemency (al-'afu), and this is the best course of action. God says "And that you show clemency is closer to God-consciousness." [Al-Baqarah:237] [Al-Nahlawi p118].

3. On envy[56] (hasd)

The Prophet ﷺ said "You have been afflicted with the illness of the nations that came before you -envy and hatred. They are the shearers, I do not mean the shearers of the hair, rather they are the shearers of the religion." [At-Tirmidhi, 2510].

"When all is said and done, it should be known that envy is one of the sicknesses of the soul, and afflicts most people and from which only a few are safe from. This is why it is said, "The body is never free from envy, but debasement (i.e attachment to the lower aspects of the world) brings it out, while having a noble character hides it."

It was said to Al-Hasan Al-Basri "Can a believer be envious?" He replied, "What has made you forget Yusuf [a.s] and his brothers. May you have no father!?[57] Keep it hidden in your heart, for it will not harm you as long as it is not taken up by the hand or tongue." [Ibn Taymiyyah, Majmu Fatawa, Marad al-Qalb wa shifa'uha, V5 p77"]

3.1 The cure for envy

*"One should know that envy is one of the most critical of spiritual ailments. These cannot be treated save through both **knowledge and action**.*

__3.1.1 Beneficial knowledge__ for envy is that one be convinced that envy is detrimental in both one's spiritual as well as worldly life. It has no harmful effect on the one of whom you are envious, either in this world or the hereafter, rather they will benefit from this. When you realise this and desist from being an enemy of yourself and a friend of your enemy, you will definitely leave envy." [al-Ghazali, Ihya, v5, 701]

__3.1.2 As for beneficial action__ in this regard, it is to attain control of one's envy, so that whatever one's envy demands by way of words or action, one should demand of one's self to act opposite to that. If envy dictates criticising the object of one's envy, one forces one's tongue to praise and speak highly of that person. If the self demands that one display arrogance, one should force oneself to humility and seeking the person's pardon" [al-Ghazali, Ihya, v5, 709]

4. Imam al-Mawlud on 'the comprehensive treatment of the heart'

The ailments that can occur in the spiritual heart are many, and each has a particular cure associated with it. These cures come back to two main points. Firstly, countering the origin of the disease itself - such as a person suffering from laziness observing their food intake. Secondly, it lies in habituating oneself to doing the opposite of the disease, such as a person who is given to arrogance taking the path of developing humility in their conduct.

However, there are some comprehensive treatments mentioned by scholars that help in treating all diseases. These are mentioned by Imam Mawlud in the following lines of didactical poetry:

---

[56] *Ibn `Umar (RA) related that the Prophet ﷺ said, "There is no envy except in two cases: a person to whom God has granted wisdom, and he rules by this and teaches it to the people, and a person to whom God has granted wealth and property along with this the power to spend it in the cause of Truth."[al-Bukhari and Muslim]*

[57] Archaic Arabic phrase expressing surprise.

"A comprehensive treatment plan for the heart's diseases is to **deny the self of its desires, enjoin hunger, keep worshipful vigilance in the night, [practice] silence and meditation in private;**

also keeping company with good people *who possess sincerity, those who are emulated in their states and statements;*

and finally, ***taking refuge in the One unto whom all affairs return.*** *That is the most beneficial treatment for all of the previous diseases.*

This must be to the point at which you are like a man drowning or someone lost in a barren dessert and sees no source of succour

except for the Guardian, possessor of the greatest power. He is the One who responds to the call of the distressed". [Yusuf, Purification of the Heart, p144]

5. Fleeing to God (al-firar ila Allah)

The holy grail of cures for spiritual ailments and diseases lies in turning to the Creator and Sustainer -*fleeing to God (al-firar ila Allah)* for help in ridding oneself of the blemishes in one's heart. It is to recognise that no matter how much we try, the ultimate cure for our shortcomings will never be achieved without *tawfiq* and help from God. It is reflected in the dhikr *'Lâ ḥawla wa lâ quwwata illâ bi Allâhi al-Aliyy al-Adhim'* (There is not strength or ability except through God, the Elevated and Vast).

> **"And from each thing we have created pairs in order that you be reminded. So flee to God, for indeed I have come to you from Him as a clear warner"** [Adh-Dhariyat:49-50].

In these two translated sections, the illustrious authorities on Qur'anic commentary, Imam al-Qurtubi and Shaykh Ibn 'Ajiba discuss what the Qur'anic order *'fleeing to God'* entails. The first does so through the statements of the early Muslim sages on this section of the Qur'an, while the latter looks at the existential levels of fleeing to God according to the development of self-consciousness in people.

> *"This means 'Flee from disobedience to obedience to Him'. Ibn Abbas said "Flee to God through repenting from the wrong actions". It is also related from him that he said "Flee from Him to Him by acting in obedience to Him". Muhammed Ibn Abdillah Ibn 'Amr Ibn Uthman Ibn 'Affan said "and so flee to God, meaning leave to Mecca". Al Hussain Ibn al-Fadl said "Stay away from everything other than God, since whoever flees to other than Him will not be protected from Him".*

> *Abu Bakr ibn al-Warraq said "Flee from the obedience of the Shaytan to the obedience of the Beneficent". Al-Junayd said "The Shaytan calls to falsehood and so flee to God, and He will prevent you from it". Dhu-Nun al-Misri said "Flee from ignorance to knowledge and from ungratefulness to gratefulness". 'Amr Ibn 'Uthman said "Flee from your own selves to your Lord". He also said "Flee to what has been preordained for you from God, and do not rely upon your own volition". Sahl Ibn Abdillah said "Flee from everything 'other than God' to God."[Tafsir Al-Qurtubi, v17, p55-56]*

> *"Fleeing to God can be from five things; [1] From disbelief to belief [2] From wrong actions to obedience and repentance [3] From heedlessness (ghaflah) to [gaining] alertness through constant remembrance (dhikr) [4] From existing within the laws of nature and portions to 'doing without' (zuhd) by means of striving (mujahadah) and breaking habits [5] From witnessing the sensory (al-hiss) to witnessing the meaning (al-ma'nah) - which is the station of witnessing." [Ibn Ajiba, al-Bahr al-Madid, v7, pg 223].*

Printed in Great Britain
by Amazon

43920128R00059